Giving

BILL CLINTON

Giving

How Each of Us
Can Change the World

—

HUTCHINSON
LONDON

Published by Hutchinson 2007

2 4 6 8 10 9 7 5 3 1

Copyright © 2007 by William Jefferson Clinton

William Jefferson Clinton has asserted his right under the Copyright,
Designs and Patents Act 1988 to be identified as the author of this work

Published by arrangement with Alfred A. Knopf,
a division of Random House, Inc., USA

Frontispiece:
Photograph courtesy of the Clinton Foundation/David Scull

First published in Great Britain in 2007 by
Hutchinson
Random House, 20 Vauxhall Bridge Road,
London SW1V 2SA

www.rbooks.co.uk

Addresses for companies within The Random House Group Limited can
be found at: www.randomhouse.co.uk/offices.htm

The Random House Group Limited Reg. No. 954009

A CIP catalogue record for this book
is available from the British Library

ISBN 9780091795757 (hardback)
ISBN 9780091795764 (trade paperback)

The Random House Group Limited makes every effort to ensure that
the papers used in its books are made from trees that have been legally
sourced from well-managed and credibly certified forests. Our paper
procurement policy can be found at: www.rbooks.co.uk/environment

Mixed Sources
Product group from well-managed
forests and other controlled sources
FSC www.fsc.org Cert no. TT-COC-2139
© 1996 Forest Stewardship Council

Printed and bound in Great Britain by
Mackays of Chatham Ltd, Chatham Kent

To the dedicated staff, volunteers, partners,
and financial supporters of the
Clinton Foundation, Library, and School of Public Service,
and to the memory of Ellen Verweij, a fine Dutch nurse
who lost her life while serving in our
HIV/AIDS initiative in Lesotho

CONTENTS

INTRODUCTION

WHEN I LEFT the White House, I knew I wanted to spend the rest of my life giving my time, money, and skills to worthwhile endeavors where I could make a difference. I didn't know exactly what I would do, but I wanted to help save lives, solve important problems, and give more young people the chance to live their dreams. I felt obligated to do it because of the wonderful, improbable life I'd been given by the American people and because politics, which consumed so much of my life, is a "getting" business. You have to get support, contributions, and votes, over and over again. If you serve well, it's probably a fair trade, but no sensible person can do it as long as I did without thinking you still have to give more to balance the scales. Besides, I thought I'd enjoy it. Like many people who are fortunate to live full, rewarding lives, I reached a point in my journey where, apart from taking care of my family and being with them and my friends, what I cared most about was doing what I could to make sure people younger than me don't die before their time and aren't denied the chance to find their own fulfillment. After I narrowly escaped what could have been a fatal heart attack in 2004, I felt that way even more strongly.

This drive has led me into a wide variety of service projects, a number of which are chronicled in this book. It has also given me a far greater appreciation of the countless acts of giving I have witnessed all my life and sometimes have taken for granted. And it has convinced me that almost everyone—regardless of income, available time, age, and skills—can do something useful for others and, in the process, strengthen the fabric of our shared humanity.

Like most Americans of my generation, I first learned about giving in my church, where we were taught to tithe. Most kids my age also gave small amounts to the March of Dimes crusade against polio. After Billy Graham spoke to a racially integrated crusade in Little Rock when Central High School was closed in the fight over desegregation in 1958, I sent a small portion of my allowance to his ministry for a few months. In my teens, I did the usual volunteer work associated with school activities and helping the needy around Thanksgiving and Christmas.

When I was in my first year of college, I gave a little time to a community project Georgetown University ran in poor neighborhoods in Washington, D.C., and contributed to the occasional good cause, but I dedicated most of my free time to friends and campus activities. During my last two years of college, at Oxford, and at Yale Law School, I became obsessed with politics and gave very little time or money to anything else.

After I went home to Arkansas to teach law, I did some pro bono legal work and began to make small contributions to causes I was interested in. During the years I served as governor, I tried to set aside 10 percent of my income for giving: for my church, my alma maters, and worthy local projects like a shelter for abused women and children in our neighborhood. Because I was involved in politics from 1974 on, I didn't give much time to other things.

Hillary was a different story. When I met her in law school, she was involved with a local project to provide legal services to poor people. She took an extra year to study the special needs of children at the Yale Child Study Center and the university hospital. When she graduated, she decided not to pursue prestigious and more lucrative law firm opportunities and went to work for the Children's Defense Fund to help poor children. When she came to Arkansas to be with me and taught in the law school, she ran the legal aid clinic and prison project. After we married and moved to Little Rock, while I was attorney general and governor, she cofounded the Arkansas Advocates for Children and Families; served on the board of our Children's Hospital and helped with its fund-raising drive (it became one of the nation's ten largest children's hospitals in a state with only 2.8 million people); brought an excellent preschool program from Israel to poor families in our state; headed a task force that increased access to health care for people in small towns and rural areas; and chaired a committee that developed higher standards for our schools. She also served on an American Bar Association commission on the status of women in the profession. Somehow she made time for all these volunteer efforts while she was working full-time as a lawyer, active in her local church, and fully involved in all Chelsea's school and extracurricular activities. My wife was my first role model for what it means to be a public servant without public office.

Hillary did the things she did because she wanted to make a difference. And she did them because it made her happy to see another baby in a small town get health care, another young child smiling at her preschool graduation ceremony, another student from a rural school become the first in his family to go to college, another woman break through the glass ceiling at a law firm.

Introduction

Now that we've switched places and I do public service as a private citizen, it's the human impact that I find most rewarding too. I've included one picture in this book, opposite the title page, that says it all. It captures the beautiful face and bright eyes of a Cambodian orphan born with HIV. Basil was ten months old when this photo was taken. His mother died when he was only one month old, and her doctor arranged for him to be taken in by New Hope for Cambodian Children, an organization that cares for HIV-positive orphans and other vulnerable children. When Basil arrived at the home, he was six weeks of age and had both HIV and tuberculosis. His doctor, a Clinton Foundation fellow, treated him for both conditions, giving Basil lifesaving pediatric AIDS medication through my foundation's partnership with UNITAID, which funds our efforts to treat children across the globe. Basil responded well to the treatment, gained weight, and, as you can see, is now healthy. He has a chance. That's often all one person can give another. But it can make all the difference.

I wrote this book to encourage you to give whatever you can, because everyone can give something. And there's so much to be done, down the street and around the world. It's never too late or too early to start. In this book you'll encounter givers old, young, and in between, rich, poor, and in between, highly educated, virtually illiterate, and in between. You'll read about innovative organizations, about new ways of giving time and money, and about old-fashioned acts of individual generosity and kindness. I think you'll find people with whom you can identify, groups you might want to join, companies you might want to buy from, projects you might want to start on your own. It is impossible to mention all the individuals and organizations doing good work in America and around the world. There are millions of them. Naturally, many of those I mention in this book I happen to know personally, through the work of my foundation, but I hope the people and groups profiled are diverse and representative enough to persuade you that everyone can and should be a giver.

As you read about a wide range of givers—from Bill Gates to McKenzie Steiner, a six-year-old girl who organized a drive to clean up the beach in her community—I hope you'll think about what you yourself can do. You'll find information about how to get involved with the efforts described in the book or with other people doing the same kind of work, and you'll find suggestions for doing something on your own or with your friends and neighbors. If you are especially interested in particular issues not covered, you'll also find Web sites that will put you in touch with NGOs—nongovernmental organizations—working on them.

Martin Luther King once said, "Everyone can be great because everyone can serve." I wrote this book to profile some great people and to encourage you to join their ranks.

Giving

ONE

The Explosion of Private Citizens Doing Public Good

———

IN EVERY CORNER of America and all over the world, intelligence and energy are evenly distributed, but opportunity, investment, and effective organizations aren't. As a result, billions of people are denied the chance to live their lives to the fullest, and millions die needlessly every year.

Because we live in an interdependent world, we cannot escape each other's problems. We are all vulnerable to terror, weapons of mass destruction, the spread of disease, and the potentially calamitous effects of climate change. The fact that one in four people who die this year will succumb to AIDS, tuberculosis, malaria, or infections related to dirty water casts a pall over all our children's future. As long as more than 100 million children in poor countries are not enrolled in school, there will be political and social instability, with global implications. There is a growing backlash against the global economy in both rich and poor nations where the economic growth it has stimulated has not been broadly shared. About half the world's people still live on less than $2 a day. In the

United States we have had five years of economic growth, worker productivity increases, and a forty-year high in corporate profits, but median wages are flat, and the poverty rate among working families has risen, as has the percentage of people without health insurance. Increased outsourcing of production and services has intensified insecurity. Most of the economic gains of this decade have gone to those people with the top 10 percent of incomes. And amidst all our wealth, there are people who are hungry, homeless, jobless, ill, disabled, desperate, isolated, and ignored. There are children with dreams that will die without a helping hand.

The modern world, for all its blessings, is unequal, unstable, and unsustainable. And so the great mission of the early twenty-first century is to move our neighborhoods, our nation, and the world toward integrated communities of shared opportunities, shared responsibilities, and a shared sense of genuine belonging, based on the essence of every successful community: that our common humanity is more important than our interesting differences.

Many of the problems that bedevil both rich and poor nations in the modern world cannot be adequately addressed without more enlightened government policies, more competent and honest public administration, and more investment of tax dollars. There is plenty of evidence that more effective government can produce higher incomes, better living conditions, more social justice, and a cleaner environment across the board. But in many areas, regardless of the quality of government, a critical difference is being made by citizens working as individuals, in businesses, and through nongovernmental nonprofit organizations. An NGO is any group of private citizens who join together to advance the public good.

When I left the White House in 2001, I hoped that

through my foundation I could make such a difference and keep working to move our nation and the world away from poverty, disease, conflict, and climate change. I wanted to use my time, experience, and contacts to help in saving lives, solving problems, and empowering more people to achieve their goals.

For example, in 2002 the Clinton Foundation launched an HIV/AIDS initiative (CHAI), to help developing nations deal with AIDS by setting up effective health systems, including diagnosis, care, and treatment, and by providing vital antiretroviral medicines and essential testing at the lowest costs in the world.

Last year, in the Bahamas, the first country to participate in our effort, I had a reunion with two five-year-old twin girls and a spunky eighteen-year-old boy who were desperately ill when I first met them but are healthy now because of the low-cost medicine purchased through our project. Three years ago I learned of a Haitian girl who was so weak with AIDS she had to be carried to her desk at school; she was among the first to receive medicine when we went to work there. I have a recent picture of her standing tall and radiant in a formal dress. I have seen infants in Zanzibar, played with children from Yunnan Province in China, and held orphans in Cambodia who are receiving lifesaving medicine though our AIDS initiative. Our program now works in twenty-five countries to diagnose, test, and care for people with HIV/AIDS, and forty-four more nations are able to buy low-cost drugs and testing materials under our contract. As of mid-2007, about 750,000 more people are receiving treatment purchased under CHAI agreements, representing about a third of all those in the developing world receiving treatment today.

Our effort is only one of the tens of thousands of public-service projects now being pursued by NGOs, individuals, and businesses throughout the world. It is no accident that in 2005, *Time* magazine named as its persons of the year Bill and Melinda Gates and Bono, three people who hold no political office but have done great public good as private citizens. Among its wide-ranging good works, the Bill and Melinda Gates Foundation has spent more than a billion dollars on health care in Africa and India, hundreds of millions to develop an AIDS vaccine and a preventive microbicidal gel, and more than $1.7 billion in the United States to develop globally competitive high schools. In 2000, Bono spearheaded an international movement to forgive the debts of the poorest countries. In 2005, he generated public support for British prime minister Tony Blair's successful effort to secure a commitment from the world's wealthiest nations to double aid to Africa and provide more debt relief. Today Bono is leading the ONE Campaign to enlist millions of Americans to support an investment of one percent of our gross domestic product to eliminate extreme poverty in the world.

In 2002, President Jimmy Carter won the Nobel Peace Prize, largely for his work after leaving the White House in fighting to eradicate guinea worm and river blindness in Africa, helping poor nations to become self-sufficient in food production, promoting human rights, building homes with Habitat for Humanity, and monitoring elections in troubled democracies to make sure that all eligible citizens can vote and that their votes are counted.

In 2006, the Nobel Peace Prize was awarded to Muhammad Yunus of Bangladesh for his pioneering work in founding Grameen Bank, which makes small loans to poor people, 97 percent of them women. In a nation with a per capita annual income of less than $500, the bank has made nearly seven million loans since 1983. Without requiring collateral or even a signed agreement, Grameen has an astonishing loan recovery rate of 98.3 percent, and has earned a profit in all but three years since it came into existence. In addition to enterprise loans at regular rates, which are financed out of its own deposits, the bank also runs life insurance and retirement savings programs, makes housing and education loans, and zero-interest loans to beggars, over 60 percent of which have already been paid off. When one of its borrowers dies, the branch manager attends the funeral and, before the burial, announces forgiveness of the outstanding debt. Perhaps most important, by early 2007, more than 58 percent of Grameen's borrowers had lifted themselves above the poverty line. Their combined activities made a significant contribution to the 6.7 percent growth Bangladesh achieved last year in spite of ongoing political turmoil.

Over the last twenty-five years, Grameen's success has inspired people all over the world. In the mid-1980s, Hillary and I raised funds to open a microcredit facility to spur development in rural Arkansas, based on the Grameen model and following the lead of ShoreBank in Chicago, which had pioneered the concept in America by making loans to local craftsmen to rehabilitate run-down buildings in a distressed area of Chicago's South Side. During my White House years, I secured funds from Congress to support microcredit programs and establish community development banks in the United States, and to provide about two million microcredit loans a year in developing countries.

Today, millions of loans are being made every year by microcredit institutions funded by governments, banks, businesses, wealthy individuals, and NGOs. In mid-2007, the Department for International Development in the United Kingdom announced a plan to get banking and microcredit for half the world's poorest people. Meanwhile, Opportunity International Australia, with support from the Gates Foundation, is giving all the clients of its microcredit bank in Malawi Malswitch cards that have fingerprint identification embedded on a chip to guarantee safe and secure access to credit for clients who aren't literate. The cards will help Malawi reach the critical mass necessary not just to improve individual lives but to lift regional and national economies.

In 2004, the Nobel Peace Prize was awarded to another citizen activist, Wangari Maathai of Kenya, the first East African woman to earn a doctoral degree. She tells her story in her beautifully written memoir, *Unbowed*. Thirty years ago, she began a tree-planting effort to promote soil and water conservation, sustainable development, the empowerment of women, good governance, and peace. It grew into the Green Belt Movement, which has helped Kenyan women plant more than 30 million trees; then into the Pan African Green Network, which spread her model of conservation and community building across the continent; and finally into the Green Belt Movement International, which seeks to plant one billion trees over the next decade. In the last few years, Maathai has also launched initiatives to promote waste reduction and increased recycling; to protect the endangered Congo Basin forest ecosystem; and to use conservation to help achieve the U.N. Millennium Development Goals.

The accomplishments of Muhammad Yunus and Wangari Maathai are both unique and representative of a global floodtide of NGO activity. In the United States, such citizen activism is older than our republic. Benjamin Franklin organized the first volunteer fire department in Philadelphia in 1736, forty years before our Declaration of Independence. In 1835, Alexis de Tocqueville, in *Democracy in America*, noted the eagerness of Americans to band together in community groups to attack common problems, comparing it favorably to the inclination of Europeans to depend on the state to solve them. The Red Cross, the United Way, and our civic clubs have been around a long time.

What makes the current movement remarkable is the sheer number and global sweep of such efforts, from the multibillion-dollar Gates Foundation to groups like the Self Employed Women's Association in India, which makes small loans to poor village women to start or expand businesses.

There are several reasons for this explosion of citizen service. First, since the end of the Cold War, for the first time in history a majority of the world's people are living under elected governments, which create more opportunities for democratic societies and citizen activism to develop. And because of the global mass media culture and leaders' unavoidable sensitivity to public opinion, even nondemocratic governments find it increasingly difficult to prevent people from organizing for advocacy or action. When I became president in 1993 there were virtually no NGOs in Russia or China. Today, even though President Vladimir Putin has severely restricted them, Russia has more than 400,000. China has almost 280,000 NGOs registered with the government, and perhaps twice that number unregistered. India, a democracy born out of Gandhi's citizen activism, has more than 500,000 working NGOs. The United States has more than one million charitable organizations, twice as many as in 2000. They employ 10.2 million people, 7 percent of our workforce.

Second, the information technology revolution and the globalization of commerce have produced vast new fortunes. There are more millionaires and billionaires than ever, and, fortunately, many of them want to reinvest a sizable portion of their wealth in solving problems and giving people in their own countries or people half a world away the chance to break the chains of poverty, disease, lack of education, or group hatred so that they too can live productive, peaceful, fulfilling lives.

Third, charitable giving has been democratized as never before, primarily through the Internet, enabling citizens of modest means who share a common concern to amass huge sums of money. When the tsunami hit Southeast Asia, Americans quickly gave more than $1 billion for relief. About 30 percent of our households contributed, more than half of them via the Internet. The disaster evoked a similar response in other developed nations, many of which contributed even more per capita than we did, including the United Kingdom, Australia, New Zealand, and the Scandinavian countries that lost many citizens who were vacationing in the area where the tsunami struck.

When Hurricane Katrina ravaged the Gulf Coast, President George W. Bush asked his father and me to help raise private funds to supplement the government's efforts. Shortly afterward, I made my annual trip to the New York State Fair with Hillary. As I was walking down the midway with my nephew, a woman came out from behind one of the game booths and handed me $50. She said, "This is for the Bush-Clinton Katrina Fund. I'm sorry to give you cash, but as you can see, I'm working and don't have time to send it over the Net." This working woman's preferred method of giving was via the Internet, a development inconceivable just a few years ago. When I became president in 1993 there were only fifty sites on the World Wide Web. When I left, there were 9 million. There are hundreds of millions today.

Perhaps the most unique mechanism for raising large sums in small amounts is the Dutch Postcode Lottery. Launched in 1989, the lottery is unique in two ways. Every month, and twice in July, thousands of winners are drawn. In addition to the Jackpot winner, there are street and neighborhood winners—all those who buy a ticket in the winning area share the prize. More important, 50 percent of the gross proceeds of the lottery go directly to charities, with an emphasis on those pursuing social justice, environmental protection, and development aid. It's a great deal. While individual prize winnings are smaller than in a traditional lottery, the number of winners is larger, and every Dutch citizen knows that half the proceeds of every lottery ticket will go directly to good causes. Since 1989, the lottery has given more than 2.3 billion euros ($3.1 billion), more than 217 million euros in 2006, to scores of NGOs, including Doctors Without Borders, Oxfam, the World Wildlife Fund, Amnesty International, and Greenpeace. It has also supported the work of my foundation and our work on climate change.

The impact of these three trends—the growth of civil society in the developing world, the vast pool of new wealth available for giving, and the rising influence of small donors—has been reinforced by the proven ability of NGOs of all sizes and missions to have a positive effect on problems at home and abroad, often in partnership with governments and local NGOs in developing countries. Still, both the potential and the need for further advances are enormous, largely due to the staggering scale of global poverty and underdevelopment, and the persistence of pockets of poverty and other social problems in the United States and other developed nations.

I thought I could help meet that challenge by convening the first Clinton Global Initiative around the annual opening of the United Nations General Assembly, in September 2005. We brought together several hundred government leaders, philanthropists, business leaders, and NGO activists from all over the world to discuss what we could do about four global challenges: combating climate change; alleviating extreme poverty; improving governance in poor nations; and promoting religious, ethnic, and racial reconciliation. The unique thing about this gathering was that the participants were told in advance that they would be asked to make a specific commitment in time or money to one of these areas. For three days, we held intense discussions about the issues; collected many good new ideas as well as examples of successful projects that should be expanded; and secured more than $2.5 billion in pledges to take specific actions. All but fourteen of the individuals and groups who attended made commitments. In dollar terms, some were large, some were small, but all will make a difference.

At the second meeting, in September 2006, the total commitments exceeded $7 billion to fight poverty, improve health, combat climate change, and promote reconciliation— with some of the most impressive pledges involving smaller dollar amounts. We now have a full-time staff to help those who make commitments keep them effectively, to assist those who have good ideas but need to find funding partners, and to match people who want to give money with reliable partners to do the work they want to finance. We also webcast the 2006 meeting. About 48,000 people followed it over the Internet, and a few hundred of them spontaneously made their own commitments. I want to continue these meetings for at least a decade, with the objective of creating a global network of citizen activists who reach across the divides of our interdependent world to build real communities of shared opportunities, shared responsibilities, and a genuine sense of belonging. You can be one of those activists, helping to build that kind of world in an almost infinite number of ways.

TWO

Giving Money

———

ABOUT 70 PERCENT of American households and increasing numbers of people around the world give some money away every year. In 2006, Americans gave almost 2 percent of our GDP (Gross Domestic Product), about $300 billion, usually in one of three categories: to their place of worship or its affiliated activities; to an emergency with profound and highly publicized needs, like the tsunami, Hurricane Katrina, or a sick child in their community who needs surgery the family can't afford; or to other local fund-raising activities by a group in which the donor is involved or to which the donor is asked to give by a friend or family member.

What if you want to go beyond that, to make a gift within your means to tackle persistent problems in the United States or other countries? The most colossal example of this sort of giving is, of course, the Bill and Melinda Gates Foundation. The Gateses decided to put more than $35 billion into a foundation to address a wide range of global issues, focusing on education in the United States and health care in poor countries, and on creating breakthroughs in deploying new vaccines and preventive measures against AIDS, other diseases, and extreme poverty. They have a brilliant staff and fund promising projects and proven partners. Both Bill and Melinda are deeply involved in the foundation's work, amazingly knowledgeable about the problems they're tackling, and intensely committed to making a difference. Bill is in the process of disengaging from Microsoft and soon will join Melinda in devoting himself full-time to their foundation.

Why did the Gateses decide to give their money and time to reducing the world's inequalities in health, education, and development? In his Harvard commencement speech on June 2, 2007, Bill Gates gave a powerful answer:

If you believe that every life has equal value, it's revolting to learn that some lives are seen as worth saving and others are not. We said to ourselves: "This can't be true. But if it is true, it deserves to be the priority of our giving."

So we began our work in the same way anyone here would begin it. We asked: "How could the world let these children die?"

The answer is simple, and harsh. The market did not reward saving the lives of these children, and governments did not subsidize it. So the children died because their mothers and their fathers had no power in the market and no voice in the system.

But you and I have both.

We can make market forces work better for the poor if we can develop a more creative capitalism—if we can stretch the reach of market forces so that more people can make a profit, or at least make a living,

serving people who are suffering from the worst
inequities. We also can press governments around the
world to spend taxpayer money in ways that better
reflect the values of the people who pay the taxes.

If we can find approaches that meet the needs of
the poor in ways that generate profits for business and
votes for politicians, we will have found a sustainable
way to reduce inequity in the world.

This task is open-ended. It can never be finished.
But a conscious effort to answer this challenge will
change the world.

The Gates Foundation follows a simple formula in
investing its massive wealth to make the most of Bill and
Melinda's determination to reduce inequity: identify problems; find solutions; measure the impact of the work in
human terms "so people can feel what saving a life means to
the families affected"; and share the successes and failures
"so that others learn from your efforts."

It's a good game plan for all giving, though easier said
than done. At a White House conference on philanthropy
that Hillary and I sponsored in 2000, Bill Gates made a state-
ment I'll never forget: "It may be harder to give this money
away than it was to make it." Warren Buffett, America's
second-wealthiest man, solved the problem in a unique way:
he decided to give the bulk of his fortune, some $30 billion,
to the Gates Foundation. He is also giving sizable sums to
the foundations of each of his children: Susie, Howard, and
Peter, all of whom have their own admirable philanthropic
activities. When I called Warren to congratulate him on his
gift, I asked what had prompted him. With his no-nonsense
Midwestern practicality he said, "I got rich because investors
thought I could make more investing their money than they

could. Bill and Melinda can spend my money better than I could." Most people of Buffett's wealth and stature would have established their own programs and funded applicants in their own names. It's a real tribute to Buffett that after he saw all the good his friends were doing, he decided to maximize the good his money will do by entrusting it to them.

When I questioned Buffett further about why he decided to give almost all his money away, he said, "My gift is nothing. I can have everything I need with less than one percent of my wealth. I was born in the right country at the right time, and my work is disproportionately rewarded compared to teachers and soldiers. I'm just giving back surplus claims that have no value to me but can do a lot for others. The people I really admire are the small donors who give up a movie or a restaurant meal to help needier people." If we all thought and acted like Buffett, we'd live in a very different world.

Another impressive example of giving similar to the Buffett model is the Robin Hood Foundation, founded in the late 1980s by hedge fund manager Paul Tudor Jones. It has raised more than $1 billion from wealthy donors who trust Robin Hood to spend their money to fight poverty in New York City. They have good reason to do so. First, the foundation has an impressive board, including GE CEO Jeffrey Immelt; Goldman Sachs chairman Lloyd Blankfein; Dirk Ziff, chairman of Ziff Brothers Investments; entertainment executives Harvey Weinstein and John Sykes; Tom Brokaw, Diane Sawyer, and Gwyneth Paltrow. Second, the board members completely cover administrative costs, so that all donations go directly to anti-poverty efforts in four core areas: early childhood and growth; education; jobs and economic security; and survival. Finally, Robin Hood rigorously evaluates the two-hundred-plus programs it funds, from charter schools to housing for the homeless to job training for former prison inmates to the comprehensive child development initiative of the Harlem Children's Zone.

Robin Hood is a model that could and should be replicated in every city with poverty problems and well-to-do citizens who want to give to efforts that produce measurable results. Kitchen Table Charities Trust, a British NGO, offers similar opportunities to givers at all levels, collecting funds and allocating them to groups doing good work. I hope others will follow suit. San Francisco has already established a similar operation.

In the United Kingdom, hedge fund manager Arpad Busson founded ARK (Absolute Return for Kids) to give wealthy donors the chance to invest in his venture-philanthropy projects: high-performance inner-city schools and programs to support AIDS patients in South Africa and orphans in Romania. British philanthropist Richard Caring also raises large sums of money to increase protection and support for vulnerable children.

For people who can give modest amounts of money but want to follow the Buffett–Robin Hood practice of giving it to someone they trust to spend it well, Oprah Winfrey's Angel Network is a good option. Oprah uses her enormous popularity and influence to publicize and hold accountable worthy projects and invites people who can give even small amounts of money to support them. To ensure that all the donations go to "help underserved people rise to their own potential," Oprah covers the management, fund-raising, and other operating costs.

Since 1998, Oprah's Angel Network has received more than $50 million in donations, averaging just over $150 and ranging from $5 to $1.4 million; funded sixty schools in thirteen countries in Africa, Latin America, China, and Haiti;

provided $15 million in relief funds after Hurricane Katrina; given thousands of poor South African children school uniforms, shoes, and school supplies; supported community organizations helping orphaned children in three African countries; and helped women in post-conflict areas to put their lives back together. The network has also given more than $6 million in Use Your Life Awards to fifty-four small- and medium-sized organizations to expand their own efforts to help people in need, and provided books for children in nations where an Oprah's Book Club selection is set: China, Russia, Colombia, Mexico; and in Georgia, Arkansas, Alabama, and the Gulf Coast area hit by Katrina.

On top of all that, Winfrey gave $40 million of her own money to fund a new foundation to establish the Oprah Winfrey Leadership Academy for Girls, a school for academically gifted but economically disadvantaged girls in South Africa. The academy will change the lives of many young women and further increase the confidence of modest donors that Oprah's foundation will spend their money well.

I asked Oprah why she started the Angel Network and her academy. Her reply: "I wanted to give back what I was given, a sense of worth. Everyone wants to matter. Three nuns I didn't know made me feel like I mattered when my mother, half brother, half sister, and I were on welfare and they brought us food and toys for Christmas. The best gift wasn't the toys. It was being able to give an honest answer when the other kids asked what I got for Christmas." That explains the Angel Network. What about the academy? "Caring teachers made education an open door for me. I wanted to help girls like me, economically disadvantaged, but not poor in mind or spirit." Together the academy and the Angel Network brought her "the greatest joy I've ever had. I am glad I am able to help others, but what they've done for me is greater than I could have imagined."

In the fall of 2007, Oprah will introduce a new kind of reality TV show on ABC. It's called *The Big Give*. Ten contestants will be given money and an assignment. They'll film their efforts to raise more money and spend it on others. The winner will be the one who's the biggest giver. As Oprah said, "It's a unique casting call. We're looking for givers."

A few years ago, when Oprah announced that her show would focus on positive stories instead of the negative and superficial judgmentalism that dominates so much of TV, radio, and print media, a lot of people thought her ratings would dip. She made a bet that the American people want something better. So far, she's winning.

PEOPLE WHO WANT more hands-on involvement with their giving have options that fall between the comprehensive involvement of the Gates Foundation and the no-strings giving of Buffett, Robin Hood, and Angel Network donors. Every person who sets up a family foundation and makes decisions about what projects to fund does this to some extent. Universities, fine-arts organizations, and major health groups like the American Heart Association receive much of their funding from such sources.

But for people who want to make a measurable difference in a specific area, the foundation as NGO offers limitless possibilities. I have had personal experience with several outstanding examples of this kind of effort. Here are four of them.

In 2004, Chris Hohn set up a unique hedge fund in London. He called it the Children's Investment Fund and specified that a portion of the fees generated by the fund would be put into its charitable branch, the Children's Investment Fund Foundation. With very high returns on investment, the fund has already put well over a billion dollars into its

foundation. The rapidly growing operation is run by Jamie
Cooper-Hohn, Chris's wife, who brings intelligence, inten-
sity, and a businesslike insistence on results to the foundation's mission: improving the lives of poor children in
developing countries by supporting strategies that will have
a lasting positive impact on their lives and communities. The
foundation supports projects that address children with
HIV/AIDS; emergency needs of children and families
affected by war and natural disaster; microfinance; and sex-
ual exploitation. To date, most of its efforts have been
directed toward helping children with HIV/AIDS in African
countries and India, and children at risk in Darfur.

In 2005, the Hohns forged a partnership with my foundation's HIV/AIDS Initiative to provide antiretroviral medicines—ARVs—to children. At the time, more than 500,000
children under fifteen were dying of AIDS every year, and at
most only 25,000 children were receiving pediatric medicines, most of them in Brazil and Thailand where the governments provide the ARVs, leaving about 10,000 children
receiving appropriate medicine in the entire rest of the
developing world. In other words, a child with AIDS in a
poor country had a one in twenty chance of receiving lifesaving medicines (at the time the comparable figure of adults
was about one in eight). While we had succeeded in lowering
the price of adult generic ARVs to $139 per year, comparable
pediatric medicine cost $600, because of the low demand.
Most countries couldn't afford to buy them, and some tried
to make do by cutting the adult pills in half, which didn't
work very well. After meeting with Ira Magaziner—he's the
chairman of our HIV/AIDS Initiative, and I'll tell you more
about his activities later—Jamie and Chris committed to
providing medicine for ten thousand children in China,
India, and several African nations, doubling the number of

children getting treatment. The money they provided from the Children's Foundation and some of its generous friends enabled Ira to negotiate a reduction in the price to $196, setting off a surge in funding for kids and further price reductions in pediatric medicine. Meanwhile, a lot of children are going to live and have better lives because of Chris Hohn and Jamie Cooper-Hohn. And they're barely forty years old; their best work is still to come.

When I asked Chris why he was giving on such a scale, he said, "Beyond a certain point, which we'd reached, money has no further value. It can't bring happiness, but it can save or transform many lives." He said he had wanted to help children since he had worked as a young man in the Philippines, where he saw kids as young as five scouring garbage dumps for food. Jamie told me they were also "concerned about the values our own children grow up with. We want them to be kind, to care about others and give them dignity, to make good things happen." They both said their good fortune was due in part to when and where they were born, not entirely due to their own ability, and therefore they have a "moral obligation to balance the scale." Chris and Jamie agree with Bill and Melinda Gates that "every life has equal value." Therefore, they can't be happy unless they act accordingly, and "we'd rather die happy than rich." In other words, as Jamie said, quoting the great Texas humorist Jim Hightower, "I never saw a hearse pulling a U-Haul."

Sterling Stamos, an investment firm with more than $3.5 billion under its management, combines its finance and philanthropy operations under the slogan "doing well by doing good." Each year, approximately 10 percent of the general partners' profits are allocated to social investment programs. Sterling Stamos's Corporate Philanthropy section is overseen by two brothers: Chris Stamos, a partner and former

COO of Sterling Stamos, is president, and Basil Stamos, a San Francisco physician who also works at a clinic serving a predominately homeless population, is chairman.

The primary focus of the Stamoses' giving is global health. Because ten million children die each year of preventable, curable, and treatable diseases, they see global health as a "moral opportunity" and an undervalued asset that, if properly funded, could yield a huge social benefit as well as an economic return on investment.

The first large commitment they made was to the Angkor Hospital for Children in Cambodia, one of the poorest countries in Southeast Asia with one of the highest rates of HIV, a high infant mortality rate, and a very high rate of amputees, the awful legacy of the Khmer Rouge's bloody rule in the 1970s and the land mines they left behind.

Late in 2006, I visited the hospital with Chris and Basil. It was founded in 1999 as a pediatric teaching hospital by the NGO Friends Without a Border. The Stamos brothers are the primary donors to the hospital, which sees 300 to 400 children every day and trains about 800 government health workers and students every year. While the current director is an expatriate, 98 percent of the staff is Cambodian. The Stamos brothers got involved in our HIV/AIDS Initiative in order to secure quality children's ARVs at low prices and to help scale up the treatment program. The hospital has provided care and treatment to more than 370 children with AIDS.

After Chris Stamos accompanied me on a trip to Africa, Sterling Stamos also committed $250,000 to our work in Rwanda with Partners In Health.

Why do the Stamos brothers do it? They clearly love their philanthropic work, but they also believe that it's good business. Chris says, "Ideas are what change the world, and 'meaning' is the greatest undervalued asset in the market-

place of ideas." He says that at Sterling Stamos, philanthropy adds to staff morale and productivity, gives clients a
greater sense of fulfillment, and increases the firm's financial
capital through the appeal of good works and the stimulation
of intellectual capital. Like Chris Hohn and Jamie Cooper-
Hohn, Chris and Basil Stamos are still young, with big plans
for the future, including an expansion of their health efforts
into Haiti and the Dominican Republic, and the establishment of the Archimedes Fund to invest the funds of other
NGOs, family foundations, and endowments for greatly
reduced fees, and in so doing increase dramatically the
amount of wealth available for philanthropy.

Lance Armstrong is convinced that in addition to world-
class care, he survived his battle with cancer because of the
physical fitness, mental toughness, and positive attitude that
made him the world's greatest cyclist. He wanted to give
other people with cancer a better chance to survive by
empowering them with the same skills he brought to the battle. Since 1997, the Lance Armstrong Foundation has given
millions of dollars to support cancer-survivorship programs
and initiatives, including survivorship centers across the
United States; collaborations with organizations focused on
addressing the special needs of young adults with cancer;
educational and outreach programs with more than two hundred partners like Fertile Hope, CancerCare, and the Office
of Native Cancer Survivorship; a national action plan with
the Centers for Disease Control to help the public health
community work with survivors; and support and education
to people facing the disease through its Web site and direct
assistance program, LIVESTRONG SurvivorCare. In addition to the money Armstrong himself has contributed, the
foundation's activities are supported by 15,000 volunteers
who help raise funds and by individuals who buy the famous
yellow LIVESTRONG wristbands. Fifty-five million people

across the world have worn one to support people living with cancer. Armstrong has made the most of his harrowing brush with death, not only by giving his money and knowledge, but by giving millions of people like you the chance to help by purchasing the little yellow band for a dollar.

My next example is not young in years, but his enthusiasm and imagination would do credit to someone half his age.

Lewis Cullman, eighty-eight, pioneered the leveraged buyout more than forty years ago. As one of America's first venture capitalists, he amassed a sizable fortune, much of which he and his wife, Dorothy, decided to give away during their lifetime. So far they have given more than $200 million to causes they care about. Many are established initiatives that can always use more money, like the New York Public Library, the American Museum of Natural History, the Museum of Modern Art, the Neuroscience Institute, Human Rights Watch, the Enterprise Foundation (for low-income housing), and his alma mater, Yale. But one of his causes, Chess-in-the-Schools, is a classic example of a very good idea with no chance of becoming a reality without private support.

In 1986, a couple of fellow chess enthusiasts started Chess-in-the-Schools, believing that the game's complex rules and requirements of strategy and imagination could stimulate intellectual growth in students in low-performing schools. The program was first introduced into a few New York City schools. When the Chess-in-the-Schools kids were tested on national standardized exams, they showed significant gains in reading, outperforming not only the average scores in their school districts but the national average as well. The participating students were not selected for aptitude. If the program is introduced into the second grade of a school, all second graders are taught chess.

Playing chess helps students develop thinking and analyzing skills, concentration, greater self-control, and self-confidence. The program costs about $100 a student per year. Today, Chess-in-the-Schools involves about 27,000 elementary and junior high school students in 109 schools in New York City neighborhoods with incomes low enough to qualify for the federal school lunch program. It also operates after-school programs in more than 110 schools, and sponsors weekend and holiday tournaments and four citywide tournaments with up to one thousand participants. There is an alumni program that helps high school students prepare for and gain admission to college.

Early on, Lewis gave the program $1 million. Now he helps raise money for it from corporations, foundations, and individuals, and convinces people like me to attend events to increase its visibility. Despite the growth of Chess-in-the-Schools, there are almost one hundred schools on a waiting list. Every year, results of national reading tests show poor students behind their more well-off contemporaries, without the reading skills necessary to succeed in an information technology economy. We have hard evidence that Chess-in-the-Schools works, for $100 a student. Our kids need more Lewis Cullmans, or a lot more people who will give $100.

The $100 option brings me to the last, and potentially most important, giver in this chapter: you. The vast majority of you who read this book can't give anywhere near the amounts the Hohns, the Stamos brothers, and the Cullmans do. But if all of you searched your heart for the causes you really care about and gave what you could to them, the aggregate amount and its effect would be significant. Many people work for businesses that match their employees' contributions. It's a great way to double the impact of your gift.

BECAUSE I GREW UP in a family without a lot of money, in a place where most families had to watch how they spent every penny, I've always respected people who found a way to give when it isn't easy to do. The most astonishing example of this kind of giving I ever saw occurred in 1995, when Oseola McCarty, an eighty-seven-year-old black woman from Hattiesburg, Mississippi, gave $150,000 to the University of Southern Mississippi to endow a scholarship fund for African-American students in financial need.

For more than seventy-five years Oseola McCarty had eked out a living washing and ironing other people's clothes. She dropped out of school in the sixth grade to take care of her sick, childless aunt and never returned. She never married. From 1947 on, she lived in a modest home her uncle gave her. She never owned a car and at eighty-seven still walked over a mile to the nearest grocery store to buy food, pushing her own shopping cart. All this time she was saving, and her savings were earning interest in the local bank. At the end of 1994, the arthritis in her hands forced her to give up washing and ironing. She met with her banker and decided that she wanted to give 60 percent of her savings to help deserving young people go to college, with the rest going to her church and relatives.

In August 1995, Stephanie Bullock, an eighteen-year-old Hattiesburg High School honor student, won the first Oseola McCarty scholarship. The next month Oseola took a train to Washington, D.C., where she was honored at the annual banquet of the Congressional Black Caucus. A couple of days later, I welcomed her to the White House and presented her with the Presidential Citizens Medal. Meeting Oseola McCarty was a real treat. Intelligent, articulate, and straightforward, she clearly enjoyed the recognition Washington gave her, but wasn't carried away by it. She had saved all her life both because she knew the perils of being penniless and because she thought it foolish to spend on things she didn't need. She accepted the obligations life had imposed on her but wanted young people to have the educational opportunities she'd missed. In her mind, she was balancing the scales, and that was reward enough.

Most people of modest means can't save as much of their income as Oseola McCarty but are willing to give a little money every year to a good cause. Unless they contribute to a local fund-raiser, they're often unsure that their $25 or $50 will make a difference. That question has been resolved in an innovative way by Kiva, an NGO that offers people the chance to become microcredit lenders of as little as $25 to entrepreneurs in developing countries. Here's how it works. A lender goes to the Web site Kiva.org, which displays photos of prescreened people and tells you what they need money for and how much they need. The lenders make a choice and pay by credit card. Kiva then transfers the money to a local partner, which makes the loan to the business. During the period of the loan, the partner provides updates to the lender on the business's progress and collects the repayment, which the lender can withdraw from Kiva or reloan.

I first learned about Kiva at my 2006 Clinton Global Initiative. Neal, one of the hundreds of people following the webcast, wrote us to say his commitment was to help eliminate poverty in developing countries by making $25 loans to assist people featured on Kiva's Web site start-up or expand their operations. On March 27, 2007, *New York Times* columnist Nicholas Kristof described his own experience as a Kiva lender. He loaned $25 each to a TV repair shop owner and a baker in Afghanistan. The baker had received $425 from a total of seven American lenders, enough to open a second bakery. The TV repairman had also opened a second shop. Between them they had created six new jobs and, in the process, increased the chances that Afghanistan can succeed in building a moderate Muslim democracy in the face of the Taliban's efforts to undo it.

Some of the most interesting giving is being done by young people. Two Minnesota sixth graders, Rachel Floeder and Audrey Feltz, established the Kids to the Rescue Fund, set up through the Salvation Army, to help children affected by Hurricane Katrina. Their goal was to collect $1 from as many of their contemporaries as possible and to challenge kids across America to follow their example. When I was in Minneapolis in 2006, I met the student leaders of Kids to the Rescue. They had raised $24,000 for victims of Katrina.

In September 2005, Hillary worked with Commerce Bank and Future Tech Enterprise, Inc., to set up a similar effort by New York schoolchildren called Coins from Kids. In just four months, children from more than forty school districts had given $31,510.47 to Katrina recovery efforts.

There is another way young people can give money that I really like: selling a product or service for a good cause. This kind of giving goes on all over America every day. Kids' lemonade stands, student car washes, and old-fashioned pie suppers in small communities: all raise funds for worthy local projects. When I was in politics in Arkansas, one mandatory annual appearance for every politician in the state was the Gillett Coon Supper, which always drew 1,500 or more people to a town of eight hundred in the rice country of southeast Arkansas. The local high school always fielded a good football team, but it was too small to afford one, so the budget gap was filled when a crowd twice as large as the total population actually paid good money to eat barbecued raccoon! It's an experience everyone ought to have once in a lifetime—as long as there's plenty of barbecue sauce to help make the coon meat edible.

Giving Money

I recently came across a particularly compelling example of this kind of giving. Eli Winkelman, a student at Scripps College in Southern California, organized her own NGO, Challah for Hunger. Every week Challah for Hunger volunteers produce more than 150 loaves of challah, the braided bread Jews traditionally break at the beginning of the Sabbath meal or during religious services. Each Friday morning, the students sell the bread to their fellow students, on tables that also have information on the hunger crisis in Darfur, "Stop Genocide in Sudan" T-shirts, "Save Darfur" bracelets, and letter-writing and advocacy materials. Students who use the materials for "Acts of Advocacy" get a discount on their challah purchases. Every week Challah for Hunger sends at least $300 to Darfur relief efforts and generates fifty letters and postcards advocating more assistance to the refugees or more serious coverage of the crisis by the media. Since November 2004, Challah for Hunger has sent more than $20,000 from students at Scripps and the other colleges in the Claremont group.

I find this effort particularly touching and relevant because it was started by a Jewish student, and is funded by the sales of traditional Jewish bread for the benefit of poor Muslims whose plight has been ignored for too long by Muslim nations much closer to them. Eli says she got the idea for Challah for Hunger "almost by accident. I baked bread because people liked it. But I realized it was a gift to have the time and money to do it, and the only way to honor the way I've been blessed was to do something worthy." Eli graduated from Scripps in the spring of 2007, but others will continue the work there, and she is hoping to see it expanded to other college campuses. There is already a Challah for Hunger effort at the University of Texas at Austin and a similar project at the University of Massachusetts at Amherst. Eli spent the summer of 2007 in Israel working with Sudanese refugees and thinking about how "you can use purchasing power to do all sorts of good things." Eli Winkelman's Challah for Hunger business card carries this quote from Rabbi Tarfon: "You are not obligated to complete the task, but you are not free to withdraw from it."

We can learn a lot about giving from young people. Indeed, the best book I've come across on the subject was written by a young person. *A Kid's Guide to Giving* by Freddi Zeiler provides a good roadmap to giving for people of all ages. Zeiler published the book in 2006, when she was a twenty-year-old student at the University of California at Berkeley, with the support of By Kids for Kids, an organization devoted to releasing the innovative spirit within all children and helping them to become good problem solvers. Zeiler started giving money away at fourteen, and over the years learned a lot about how to develop the discipline to save enough for giving, as well as how to volunteer time, donate goods, and organize charity events. The book examines three important issues: why you should give, how to choose a cause, and how to contribute money, time, or things. It also has a useful list of charities and a clear summary analysis of the needs of people, animals, and the environment.

Last Christmas, Hillary and I gave copies of Zeiler's book to our two nephews, ages twelve and thirteen. We told them we'd send them a certain amount of money each month if they would agree to give 25 percent of it to charitable causes of their choice and write or call us each month with an account of what they supported and why; then we'd send the next installment. They both eagerly accepted the offer and are taking their responsibility seriously. So far, they've given money to the American Heart Association; Animal Rescue

Giving Money

New Orleans, which cares for and finds homes for pets left homeless by Hurricane Katrina; and Seeds of Peace, which promotes mutual respect and understanding between young Arabs and Israelis. I hope giving develops into a lifetime habit for them, and I recommend the book, and the exercise, to you.

THREE

Giving Time

———

WHILE WE DON'T all have the same amount of money, we do have access to the same twenty-four hours in every day. Though some people have much less free time than others, nearly everyone can carve out some opportunity for giving. The gift of time can sometimes be more satisfying and more valuable than money, as Americans will tell you who have volunteered at a homeless shelter or center for troubled families, brought meals on wheels to seniors or gone to the grocery store for an elderly neighbor, helped with nonmedical tasks in hospitals, tutored young students in reading or math, mentored kids from poor neighborhoods to help them prepare for college and succeed in life, served as an AmeriCorps volunteer, or stacked sandbags during a flood.

What you do with your time-giving depends on how much you have to give, what you know, and most of all, what you really care about. A treasured few give a lifetime of service to others. A few more give a year or two, usually early in life or after years of work or in retirement. Still more give a few weeks a year. Many step up in the aftermath of a natural disaster. And millions of people give an hour or so a week. In the United States, about 55 percent of American adults, almost 84 million people, give some time every year. Total time-giving exceeds the hours put in by more than nine million full-time employees, with a value of $239 billion, almost as much as the $260 billion in financial contributions Americans made in 2005. If everyone gave just the time he or she could, it would help millions of people.

One of the world's greatest full-time givers is Dr. Paul Farmer. Farmer had an interesting childhood. His father and mother never made enough money to give their six children economic security, and for most of his childhood Paul lived in the family bus in a Florida trailer park, with an extended period living on a boat and a brief stay in a tent. However, his parents gave him something more important than material goods: they encouraged his insatiable curiosity and the development of his fine mind. A lot of people who grow up with a firsthand acquaintance with poverty can't wait to escape it. Not Farmer. He wants to get rid of it, or at least its worst consequences. Even before he graduated from Duke University and then Harvard Medical School, Paul Farmer knew he would devote his life to giving high-quality medical care to the poor.

In 1987, he founded Partners In Health, along with fellow doctor Jim Yong Kim, his friend Ophelia Dahl, and Boston businessman Tom White, who put up the first $1 million to support the Zanmi Lasante Clinic that Farmer and Haitian colleagues opened in Cange in the central highlands of Haiti, the poorest nation in the Western Hemisphere, long burdened by oppressive, corrupt, and violent rulers. For the next several years, Farmer spent about four months a year practicing medicine at the Brigham and

Women's Hospital in Boston, where he earned enough to pay his bills. The rest of his time was devoted to caring for people at Zanmi Lasante and building an innovative public health-care model that holds great promise for the rest of the developing world. Farmer lived in a simple home by the clinic, with a tin roof and concrete floors, with no hot water, but with the relative luxury of a toilet.

More than 600,000 people live in the clinic's "catchment area," in small villages that are served by community health workers trained by Partners In Health. Many people from outside the area also come to the clinic because of the high quality of its care. It has about 1.7 million patient visits a year; has built schools, houses, and water and sanitation systems; has vaccinated all the children in its area; and has reduced infant mortality and malnutrition dramatically.

What brought Farmer's work worldwide notice is the progress he and his colleagues made in treating tuberculosis and AIDS. For about $150 to $200, one percent of what it costs to treat a TB patient in the United States, Partners In Health, relying on community health workers, fought TB in central Haiti to a standstill. Almost no one in the catchment area has died from TB since 1988. By the late 1990s the clinic had also reduced the transmission of HIV from infected mothers to their babies to 4 percent, as low as the rate in the United States at the time.

Over the years, Partners In Health has won support from the Global Fund to Fight AIDS, Tuberculosis, and Malaria, and George Soros, the Gates Foundation, and other private donors. The money has enabled it to expand its lifesaving work, especially in the care and treatment of people with HIV/AIDS. It also expanded its TB treatment into Russia and Peru, where it achieved particularly impressive results under the leadership of Jim Kim, who, like Farmer, has devoted his life to public health. After leaving Partners In Health, Kim went on to the World Health Organization, where he led the push for widespread treatment for people with AIDS. He is now the director of the Department of Social Medicine at Harvard Medical School and at Brigham and Women's Hospital in Boston and back with Partners In Health.

I first met Farmer in 2002 at the World AIDS Conference in Barcelona. In 2003, I joined him in Haiti to cement my foundation's partnership with the government to provide training and low-cost medicine to fight HIV/AIDS. We held an event to announce our joint efforts at a hospital in Port-au-Prince. When my interpreter proved not very adept at translating my words into Creole, Farmer politely took over for him and saved the day, a familiar role for him.

A couple of years later, Ira Magaziner persuaded Paul to try to implement the Partners In Health model in Rwanda. The health-care system there had been decimated by the 1994 genocide, in which about 800,000 people—10 percent of the population—had been slaughtered in just ninety days and where the per capita income is less than $1 a day. Partners In Health committed to scale up care in two rural provinces. Never one to do something halfway, and confident that his clinic in Haiti could now operate without him, Paul, his Haitian wife, Didi, and their young daughter, Catherine, moved to Rwanda.

In 2006, I went to Rwanda to see how things were going. Partners In Health had already completed the restoration of Rwinkwavu Hospital. Closed since the genocide, it now has an infectious disease unit, an operating room, an X-ray facility, a center for malnourished children, electronic medical records, and Internet access. Partners also had begun treatment to prevent mother-to-child transmission of HIV and worked with the Rwandan government to ensure widespread distribution of medicine to people with AIDS. It has enrolled more than 1,700 patients in its rural care model; trained over eight hundred health-care workers to treat people who can't come to the hospital or don't need to do so now; and opened five clinics in rural villages with electricity from photovoltaic cells provided by another wonderful NGO, the Solar Electric Light Fund. Together with the government of Rwanda's ministry of health, Partners In Health is renovating another hospital to serve 300,000 people and opening a center to train Rwandan health workers to provide high-quality primary care and treatment for HIV, TB, and malaria in rural areas. Partners In Health will also provide pediatric medicine to children with AIDS, and launch clean water and sustainable development projects essential to public health. If the Partners In Health's efforts are as successful in Rwanda as they have been in Haiti, there will be a model that can be implemented in every developing nation in Africa and across the world to narrow the unconscionable health divide between the world's poor and the rest of us.

I asked Paul why, after all the economic insecurity of his childhood, he wasn't content to give two or three weeks a year to caring for the poor and spend the rest of his time enjoying the financial and other rewards his skills and ability could bring. He told me that even though he grew up living in a bus with seven other people, his parents were still concerned about and generous to those with even less. Then when he moved from his bus to Duke University, he realized that he and other young Americans, no matter what their income, had great opportunities. But when he went to Haiti, he saw people living in conditions that made his bus look like a palace. Even worse, they didn't "feel they could make things better: I wanted them to know the floor in the hospital didn't have to be dirty; the women didn't have to die in childbirth. Haiti was my greatest teacher. After going there, I couldn't do anything else."

I have told Farmer's story at some length to demonstrate the incredible impact one person with a fine mind, boundless energy, and a passion for justice can have. When I first heard of Paul, I asked my daughter, who has a long-standing interest in global health issues, if she knew anything about him. She said, "Oh, Dad, he's a saint. He's our generation's Albert Schweitzer." Paul Farmer is not yet fifty. I hope to live to see him get the Nobel Prize and—more important—to inspire other bright selfless young men and women to follow in his footsteps.

THE PAUL FARMER model of giving time, like the Gates model of giving money, isn't for everyone. Most people either don't want to devote their entire lives to a particular cause or have obligations that prevent them from doing so. But just as is the case with money, many people do want to give time to causes that are important to them.

When I recovered from my heart surgery, I wanted to do something to help others avoid the same fate or worse. In May 2005, working with the American Heart Association, my foundation launched the Alliance for a Healthier Generation to halt the alarming rise of childhood obesity by 2010, then reverse it. Increasingly, childhood obesity, with all its complications, is becoming a global problem. China and India are grappling with it. There are national anti-obesity campaigns under way in Ireland, Australia, and the United Kingdom, where the National Obesity Forum is focused on involving the media in food education and on improving the quality of school food. Today, 12.5 million American children are obese, an additional 13 million are overweight, and more and more of them are developing problems normally found only in adults—high blood pressure, high cholesterol, and type 2 diabetes, which can lead to heart attacks, strokes, blindness, and loss of limbs. If childhood obesity continues to increase, this young generation could be the first in American history to have shorter lives than their parents. To get the alliance off to a good start, I asked the Republican governor of Arkansas, Mike Huckabee, to co-lead the effort with me because I wanted an inclusive, nonpartisan effort; because he had implemented a good child-health program in his state; and because he was a great example: he lost 110 pounds, got off his diabetes medicine, and ran his first marathon at age forty-nine. After Huckabee left office, Governor Arnold Schwarzenegger, who also has aggressively tackled the childhood obesity issue, became the Alliance co-leader.

Our plan called for involving industry, schools, health-care providers, and kids themselves in efforts to stop the nationwide increase in childhood obesity and to empower young people to make healthy lifestyle choices. It was a great idea but a huge, complex challenge. The American Heart Association has an extensive presence in communities and schools across America, invaluable expertise, and a national network of volunteers and supporters who give time and money, but we needed someone to organize and run this operation, someone willing to take on a big job without a big salary.

In stepped Bob Harrison. A graduate of Cornell University and Yale Law School and a Rhodes Scholar, Bob spent twenty-two years on Wall Street as an investment banker and lawyer. He became a partner at Goldman Sachs, and co-head of its Global Communications, Media, and Entertainment Group. In 2003, still a young man, he retired to pursue public service full-time. In 2004, he was involved in the presidential campaigns of General Wesley Clark and Senator John Kerry. The next year, he found his way to my foundation, where he led a task force that studied the feasibility of adding clean water and sanitation to our health and development efforts in Africa and Asia. In his spare time, he serves as chairman of the board of New York City's Henry Street Settlement, a 114-year-old anti-poverty organization that provides shelters for the homeless and for battered women, home care to seniors, mental and physical health clinics, and youth and workforce development programs.

Bob took on his new start-up with enthusiasm. Operating out of a small room in my Harlem office, he developed a compelling presentation of the problem, complete with statistics and charts, and a clear strategy for tackling it. In just a year and a half, Bob has helped broker deals with the beverage and snack food industries to stop the sale of high-calorie beverages and snacks in schools. He has started the Healthy Schools Program, a partnership with the Robert Wood Johnson Foundation, to support the development of better nutrition, more physical activity, and good staff wellness programs, and to recognize schools that enhance their health practices. The program is already in place. It has reached more than 750,000 kids in about 1,000 schools in forty-four states, with a special emphasis on low-income student populations at higher risk of obesity. Over the next four years, we hope to help thirty thousand schools, or one in four schools across the country. Bob partnered with Nickelodeon, the channel most watched by young children, to start the "Let's Just Play—Go Healthy Challenge," an on-air, online, and grassroots movement that encourages kids to plan to make their lives, schools, and communities healthier. Nickelodeon has committed more than $28 million a year in airtime and outreach to the effort. In 2006, its first year, more than 150,000 kids across America embraced Nickelodeon's "Go Healthy" challenge to lead more active, healthier lives. The program is thriving with new partnerships with Rachael Ray, the NBA, and educational TV network Channel One.

Bob Harrison doesn't make quite as much money working to save our kids as he did at Goldman Sachs, but the good he does is a rich reward.

THERE ARE MORE and more people becoming time-givers after successful careers. Dr. Consuelo Beck-Sagué came to the United States from Cuba in 1961. For twenty years she worked at the Centers for Disease Control in Atlanta, specializing in HIV, TB, hospital infections, reproductive health, and child abuse. After attending the international AIDS conference in Barcelona in 2002, she and her husband decided that when they retired, they would devote themselves to caring for people infected with the virus. The next year, they moved to the Dominican Republic, and Dr. Beck-Sagué began providing antiretroviral therapy to children and adults at her clinic in La Romana and others throughout the country. She has now seen to it that hundreds of people are, in her words, "snatched from an untimely death, and brought back to the arms of their loved ones." The doctor sent me pictures of Juan, one of her patients, the first taken in May 2005 when he started ARVs and nutritional support, weighing seventy-five pounds. In the second, taken just four months later, Juan weighs a healthy 130 pounds. He now has a full-time job and works as a volunteer caregiver.

In late 2004, Jimmy and Janet Jones came to my office in Harlem to talk about our AIDS work. They had both had interesting careers and had long been active in church and community-service activities, including a program they ran providing twenty-five to thirty college scholarships a year for minority students in New Jersey. After graduating from the University of Nebraska, Jimmy played professional football for four years, then had a successful business career with a number of companies before retiring as senior vice president and chief of human resources at Reebok International. Janet earned a doctorate in education, which led her into a thirty-five-year career as a teacher, school district administrator, and human resources consultant.

Shortly after their visit to Harlem, Jimmy and Janet agreed to become the project leaders of our HIV effort in Lesotho. A small mountain kingdom of 1.8 million people completely surrounded by South Africa, Lesotho has one of the world's highest HIV rates: about a quarter of the population is infected. Over the course of a year, the Joneses made ten two-week visits to Lesotho, and assembled a team of clinical and business experts to develop a plan for care and treatment across the country. They faced many problems, including a shortage of health-care workers, an aversion to condom use, and an infected population with severe malnourishment and a great deal of tuberculosis.

The team led by the Joneses delivered their five-year plan in May 2005. It is now being implemented, and the Lesotho government has begun an effort to test every person over twelve for HIV/AIDS. But developing a plan wasn't enough for the Joneses. They also continued their education mission, making sure children learned how to prevent the spread of HIV and even persuading my foundation to donate $35,000 to cover the fees of hundreds of high school seniors who otherwise would have been forced to drop out.

Our AIDS project in Lesotho has been given the gift of

time by others as well, local citizens who are neither wealthy nor financially secure. Their great resource is that they are HIV-positive. These "expert patients" visit all the villages, often areas so remote they're reachable only on foot or on the back of a four-legged carrier. They try to combat the stigma and fear of AIDS and to convince people to be tested so that they can get proper care and treatment and don't infect others.

One of our most effective expert patients is a remarkable twenty-three-year-old woman, Tsepang Setaka. She is beautiful, intelligent, articulate, and HIV-positive, in an environment where the infection and the way she got it might have caused her to live in isolation and shame. With a strong religious faith and wisdom beyond her years, Tsepang made a different choice. Here, in her own words, is her story, told to a group of supporters of our work in October 2006:

My name is Tsepang Setaka. I am twenty-three years old and am an expert patient in Lesotho, Africa. I am pleased to be here tonight to share my story and to tell you about the work that I am doing for the Clinton Foundation in Lesotho. October hasn't always been a good month for me. In October 2001, I was walking home from high school with a friend, and we were kidnapped. I was held hostage in a small house without windows and kept without food and water. The first day, the men said that we should sleep with them, and we refused. They threatened to kill us if we did not sleep with them. My hands were then tied with a rope, and I was repeatedly raped. The third day, a man came to check on the house and left the door open, allowing us to escape. We slept outside without blankets in the dark. The next morning we found a coin and called for help. My sister came to collect me and report our case to the police. The police accused us of lying and they refused to look into our case, even until today. When I came home, Dr. [Mphu] Ramatlapeng, a friend of my grandmother's who now runs the Clinton Foundation's program in Lesotho, tested me for many things, including STIs and pregnancy, but not HIV.

The next year, in October 2002, I was coming home from a school function and waiting for a taxi. Four boys approached me and asked me to go with them, and I declined. They forced me to go with them and beat me with sticks. They wanted to rape me. Luckily they did not succeed. The villagers came to assist me. They took me to the hospital, where Dr. Ramatlapeng once again cared for my injuries. She stitched my cuts, and I am now okay.

In October 2003, I went for my first HIV test. This was my last year of high school, and I was afraid that learning I was positive would interrupt my studies. I didn't collect the results of my test but intended to go back once school was over. Months later, after my exams, I visited the clinic to learn the results of the test. I went alone to meet the counselor, and she told me I was positive. For all of August 2004, I was coughing. I went to the hospital, and I was diagnosed with TB. I was treated for TB, and my doctor asked that I test for HIV. He didn't know that I already knew my status, and so I retested, and the test was positive.

My doctor sent me to Karabong Clinic for my HIV care. The word *Karabong* means "an answer," and people come to the Clinton Foundation knowing they will get answers. In March, my CD4 was 122, and I was started on ARVs purchased under Clinton Foundation agreements. Today my CD4 is 292. I was sick before, and now that I have started the ARVs I have become better. They have saved my life.

Before, I had bad memories about October and each year it was a month that I did not look forward to, but that has changed. Now that I am here with you in October, this is a very happy night.

In April of this year, I volunteered myself to help the other patients in Karabong Clinic. I was working in the pharmacy office and reception area. I encouraged others to test, assisted with adherence counseling and pre-ART care. I was chosen to work with the "Know Your Status" campaign, a national program that encourages people to test for HIV. I was taught how to do testing and counseling house-to-house. I continued assisting the clinic with pill counting, documentation, and adherence counseling.

I now work in Karabong Clinic as an expert patient. I am supported with a monthly stipend from the Clinton Foundation for my clinic work. I am responsible for monitoring patients who stop taking their medicine and others who need follow-up care. I am responsible for those patients who have lost hope. I encourage them by sharing my story, teaching them that HIV does not mean death but means that you can live like everyone. They have to leave the past behind them and move forward for their new lives.

People are now willing to be tested, because the drugs are there, and they know they will get the care they need, and that they will not be lost along the way.

This is my first visit to America and my first time

traveling outside of Lesotho. It was a long journey, but I was happy to make it, because I wanted to tell you my story. I look to a future of hope.

Tsepang's gift of time is priceless, not only because of the work she does, but because of the power of her example— a person who chose not to be consumed by her misfortune but to stand on its shoulders and lift others up. We now have 650 people working against HIV/AIDS around the world. None of them makes much money. And more than a hundred of them—from America, Europe, and the host countries—have worked for no salary, just transportation and room and board. Their gifts of time have helped save countless lives.

There are many well-established organizations like Doctors Without Borders and the Peace Corps that give people the chance to serve full-time for a limited period. I am particularly proud of AmeriCorps, which offers young people the chance to do one or two years of grassroots service activities, from tutoring to environmental protection to emergency response, with minimal compensation plus a grant to help defray the cost of a college education. Since it was established in 1994 under the leadership of a great social entrepreneur, the late Eli Segal, more than 500,000 people have served in AmeriCorps service programs. After I left office, I helped the largest AmeriCorps program, Boston-based City Year, to establish a branch in Little Rock, which is headquartered in one of my foundation buildings, and another in South Africa, where some two hundred white and black South Africans are building a common future by meeting today's needs. The Bush-Clinton Katrina Fund also helped create a new City Year branch in New Orleans to provide young people with a way to help the city rebuild.

After I left office, I felt so strongly about encouraging full-time givers that I worked with the University of Arkansas to establish a graduate school of public service. Located next to my presidential library, it is the only graduate school in the United States offering a masters of public service degree, which I hope will lead to service careers in the NGO, government, or private sectors. Besides the academic work, all the students participate in public-service projects ranging from local efforts in the Mississippi River Delta to international internships across the world, from Bolivia to Sudan to Vietnam. To give more young people a chance to participate in our work, Paul Orfalea, the founder of Kinko's, and his wife, Natalie, generous givers themselves, have endowed a fellowship for University of Southern California graduates in business, law, and public policy to spend a year working with my foundation in the hope that they too will be inspired to pursue long-term service careers.

MOST PEOPLE WHO want to volunteer have more limited time. For more than twenty years, the Los Angeles Conservation Corps has involved young people in community-service programs during school breaks, after school, and in response to natural disasters. For those who can give an hour or two per week, there are tutoring needs in every community that both adults and young people can meet. Adults can mentor young people as Big Brothers or Big Sisters, which have affiliates in most larger communities. Many cities and towns have parks, playgrounds, and conservation projects that need help.

Almost all facilities that serve large numbers of the general public depend heavily on volunteers. Many older Americans have more free time, and find this kind of service rewarding. Whenever I visit a hospital, I find myself looking for the senior volunteers who run the gift shops, help the visitors, and cheer the patients. Almost every large museum, art gallery, or public institution can open its doors only because volunteers enable the operations to run on budget. Even the White House couldn't answer the mail and perform other essential work without its hundreds of volunteers. My presidential library couldn't function without its more than five hundred volunteers. While they range from a seventeen-year-old to a ninety-year-old, the average age is sixty-four, and many of them are retired. They greet the visitors, conduct tours, and help with whatever problems or questions people have.

Organizations that provide services to seniors, the unemployed, the physically or mentally disabled, the homeless, recovering drug and alcohol abusers, and former prison inmates always need volunteers. Two particularly impressive examples in this category are faith-based: Project H.O.M.E. in Philadelphia, founded in 1989 by Sister Mary Scullion and Joan Dawson McConnon, and the Inter-Religious Fellowship for the Homeless of Bergen County, New Jersey. Project H.O.M.E. has grown from an emergency winter shelter for the homeless into a comprehensive effort to break the cycle of homelessness and poverty. It has created more than four hundred housing units, three businesses that employ formerly homeless people, a learning center and technology lab, and promoted an effort to improve the urban environment by greening vacant lots. I recently visited Project H.O.M.E. in North Philadelphia with Jon Bon Jovi, who has committed the funds to restore fifteen old buildings for first-time home buyers. Comcast funded the technology lab. The Saturn division of GM will make sure the buildings are green, maximizing energy efficiency and holding down utility bills. The money is important, but what makes Project H.O.M.E. work is the intense person-to-person involvement with those who want to change their lives. That takes people.

About twenty years ago, a group of Protestant, Catholic, and Jewish leaders worked together to form the Inter-Religious Fellowship for the Homeless (IRF) of Bergen County. Though one of the wealthiest counties in America, it has a sizable homeless population, including families with children and people with full-time jobs. The fellowship runs several programs: an emergency family shelter for families not eligible for or served by other programs and most often homeless because of a lack of affordable housing; a transitional program to help families regain their independence; an overflow shelter program with the support of more than sixty congregations; daily meals for up to 150 people through a "walk-in" dinner program; scholarship support for enhanced education or training that will increase job opportunities and earning potential; and a two-week summer program for thirty children for families served by the IRF.

While the fellowship raises funds for all these endeavors, it has only five paid employees. The rest of the work is done by more than four thousand volunteers whose contributions range from cooking one meal a year to staffing the office on a regular basis. For twenty years, one of the volunteers, who has thirty-seven grandchildren, has served as grandmother to the families in the shelter in addition to coordinating all the volunteer groups. Volunteers come from various congregations, social groups such as Rotary clubs and Knights of Columbus, and from the business community. High school students play with and tutor children in the family shelter and raise funds to support the summer camp. Various congregations "host" the family shelter for a week at a time, providing all the meals, and two volunteers who stay all night. They've had some amazing encounters. One volunteer, a teacher, met a single mother with four teenage daughters and a full-time job as a nurse at a New York hospital. The woman became homeless when the hospital eliminated overtime and she could no longer afford the $1,500 a month in rent on her apartment or come up with the security deposit and first month's rent for a new place. At 1 a.m. one night, the teacher found herself in the shelter correcting her students' papers while sitting next to one of the nurse's children, an honor student doing her own homework.

Because so many people live on the edge of financial insecurity, there are a lot of families like the nurse and her kids, one rent hike or health emergency away from homelessness. The commitment and cooperation exhibited by the IRF could serve as a model for religious communities around the country.

For people who can spare a few hours or a day at a time where they're needed, there's no better organization to help than Make-A-Wish. Since 1980, the Make-A-Wish Foundation has granted the wishes of more than 144,000 children around the world with life-threatening medical conditions, thanks to a network of more than 25,000 volunteers who serve as wish-givers, helpers at special events, fund-raisers, and in other capacities. The first Make-A-Wish child was a seven-year-old with leukemia who wanted to become a police officer. A U.S. Customs officer and the Arizona Department of Public Safety gave him a tour in a police helicopter, swore him in as an honorary patrolman, and made him an official uniform. The young boy died shortly afterward.

The second child, also with leukemia, wanted to be a fireman. Soon, the movement exploded to grant all kinds of wishes, including trips to Disneyland and sports events, and meeting famous people. When I was president, Make-A-Wish brought forty-seven young people to see me, either in the White House or during my visits to communities where the children lived. Those kids did a lot more for me than I did for them.

Eleven-year-old Fred Sanger from St. Louis had heart problems that required him to stay indoors a lot. He watched the news and kept up with current events. When his parents and the Make-A-Wish people brought him to see me, I was amazed at how much he knew about my work, and kept in touch with him for some time afterward. Since leaving office, I've been asked to see three more Make-A-Wish kids. One of them, eighteen-year-old Nolan Heath, came to my office in Harlem in 2006 with his parents and brothers. He had had four surgeries in the past year but still managed to enroll at the University of North Carolina Wilmington. Because I was only available during his first week of classes, he wrote to each of his professors asking for permission to miss a few classes, assuring them he was a diligent student and would quickly catch up. After I met him, I had no doubt that he would do that and more. If you want to do something that will really help children and leave you feeling good about yourself, volunteer for Make-A-Wish.

I was amazed by the number and variety of people who showed up in the Gulf Coast area to help after Hurricane Katrina. On my first trip there after the hurricane, I ran into one of Chelsea's best friends from high school, who's now an architect. He and two of his friends dropped what they were doing and traveled to Biloxi, Mississippi, for three weeks to help. And Russell Gerraerts, a Montana contractor, came to town intending to volunteer only for two weeks, and then return with his own work crew to earn some money. When he saw how bad it was, he stayed on as a volunteer.

In Pearlington, Mississippi, with no federal rebuilding funds released, insurers' paychecks delayed, and most people still living in FEMA trailers a year and a half after Katrina, homes were being rebuilt by volunteers from Habitat for Humanity, Catholics from Massachusetts, Methodists from Illinois, Amish from Pennsylvania, and other church groups from across the South.

In New Orleans, the residents of the Broadmoor neighborhood were told in early 2006 that their homes would be razed and their land turned into parks if half the residents didn't return within four months. A year later, thanks to partnerships with companies, universities, and NGOs, the residents had restored and repainted two-thirds of the 2,900 damaged homes. As of late February 2007, 55 percent of the residents had returned, and new people were moving in, with housing prices down and the neighborhood's spirit strong.

About the same time, in the Lower Ninth Ward, which was virtually wiped out by Katrina, volunteers turned the first new homes over to residents. Built of pine, elevated five feet, and designed to resist hurricane winds, the houses cost only $125,000 each. The project was organized by ACORN (Association of Community Organizations for Reform Now), which also provided the financing with support from a California bank. ACORN works to empower low- and moderate-income people through the grassroots activism of more than 200,000 members in one hundred communities all over America. The owners expect to repay the mortgage and previous loans from funds from Louisiana's Road Home project when they are released. The houses were designed with help from the Louisiana State University School of Architecture. The volunteers included university students, local church members, young people from Covenant House, and novelist Richard Ford, who recently moved back to the city and spoke at the ceremony celebrating the construction and handover. He called the occasion "a valiant and hopeful house raising," an allusion to the barn raisings of early America, where neighbors pitched in to help one another erect buildings on newly settled land. All the citizens who responded to Katrina's devastation, including many who are still working to bring back New Orleans and other communities, are part of that great tradition.

Just as with the gift of money, some of the most impressive time-givers are young people. In 1993, a once-in-five-hundred-years flood hit the heartland of America as the Mississippi River poured over its banks and levees, inundating cities, towns, and farmlands. I traveled to Des Moines, Iowa, to survey the damage, encourage the citizens, and meet with the emergency teams working to minimize the destruction and take care of the people who were flooded out of their homes. I also visited the volunteers who were stacking sandbags and delivering food and supplies. As always in such situations, all those I met were energetic, dedicated, and selfless. But one stood out. Her name was Brianne Schwantes.

A native of Kenosha, Wisconsin, Brianne had come to Iowa with her family to work in the Red Cross volunteer center and help deliver food and supplies. She was just thirteen, quite small for her age, and her body showed the effects of having been born with a rare bone disease, osteogenesis imperfecta, which made her skeleton incredibly fragile and every bone in her body vulnerable to fracture under the slightest strain. She had thirteen broken bones at birth and her doctors told her parents they didn't expect her to live through the day. But live she did, going home with her body covered with tiny casts and Popsicle-stick splints.

Her parents decided that instead of shielding Brianne from all risks, they would try to let her live a happy, healthy life, being as careful as they could, while accepting that bad things would happen. They let her be a kid and take chances, promising themselves not to blame each other when another incident occurred. Growing up, she broke the long bones in her leg about once every six months and broke toes, fingers, and ribs more frequently. By the time I met her she had undergone numerous surgeries. But she had a smile on her face, and determination in her voice. She had already testified before Congress five times to urge more funding for the National Institutes of Health, and had started *Little Bones*, a quarterly newsletter for children suffering from rare diseases, which has more than five thousand subscribers worldwide.

Brianne didn't stop giving her time after the flood. When she was fifteen, she worked with Franciscan missionaries to raise more than $25,000 for South African orphans. At eighteen, she worked as a counselor for the summer at Camp AmeriKids, a summer camp for children with HIV and other life-threatening diseases. At twenty, she co-founded and managed the first women's ice hockey team at American University in Washington, D.C. I met her again in 1999 with her college friends and was delighted to see her growing up just as her parents had hoped. Against all odds, she was a happy, healthy young woman, still deeply committed to community service.

Throughout college, Brianne volunteered with the Heart of America Foundation, speaking to more than five thousand high school and middle school students about the importance of volunteering. When she went home to Wisconsin, Brianne kept giving. At age twenty-three, she organized young women in the Wisconsin Cherry Blossom Princess program (she was the 2003 princess) to donate books and read to local schoolchildren. At twenty-four, she organized a drive in South Milwaukee that collected more than seven thousand books for children in poor rural schools. At twenty-five, in connection with Washington, D.C.'s annual Cherry Blossom Festival, she helped organize a week of activities that included a community-service project at an elementary school. Very few of us have to take the risks to serve that Brianne Schwantes takes every day. It makes her happy.

At the ripe old age of six, McKenzie Steiner organized her friends in California to participate in her second beach cleanup. She did the first beach cleanup with her school but was concerned because there was still trash on the beach when they stopped. So she decided to enlist her friends to do another one. She brought gloves and plastic bags for about twenty other kids to pick up bottle lids, containers, bags, and other trash. McKenzie told me she plans on doing a cleanup on her next birthday and several after that, and she is talking to her mother about organizing one a month. When I asked her why she did it, she said, "Sometimes animals die from people littering in the ocean. . . . I felt better for helping animals and people coming to the beach to swim."

If someone as young as McKenzie Steiner can organize her own time-giving project and someone like Brianne Schwantes can give so much, surely we all can give something.

If you're willing to volunteer, there is no shortage of organizations and projects that will be glad to welcome you. Many local newspapers run advertisements asking for volunteers who are willing to help but don't have a particular area of commitment. Or you can check out volunteermatch.org. You just put in your own zip code and it gives you a list of opportunities in your area. If you're not American or if you want to volunteer in another country, check out VSO at vso.org.uk for innovative opportunities to pass on skills to people in local communities. Whatever you do, it will almost certainly be educational, enjoyable, and rewarding. And remember, if everyone did it, we would change the world.

FOUR

Giving Things

———

Mostly individuals, families, and enterprises in wealthy countries have things they can
easily give away to people who need them, in
their own communities or around the world. The challenge
is to identify a really useful gift and get it to where it's
required or to someone who can be trusted to deliver it. Fortunately, there are some fine organizations who do that job,
most of them founded by people who saw how things that
were part of their everyday lives could make a big difference
in the lives of others.

Doc to Dock was founded by Dr. Bruce Charash to collect and deliver American medical supplies, equipment, and
pharmaceutical products to health providers in Africa and
the Middle East. More than seven thousand tons of usable
medical supplies are discarded in U.S. hospitals and clinics
every day. The organization aims to recapture as many of
these supplies as possible, solicit direct donations from manufacturers, collect supplies and equipment from doctors and
nurses at major medical conventions, and monitor the im-

pact of its donations in the hospitals and clinics that receive them. For example, Doc to Dock will ask doctors to bring an extra stethoscope to a cardiology convention, or material for plastic casts to an orthopedic meeting. Hospitals use many items that come in multi-product packages, and though each item is separately packaged, rules often prohibit the later use of items in the big package that weren't used when it was opened. Doc to Dock wants them. The organization is also creating an online market so that hospitals in Africa and the Middle East can keep up with its inventories and order exactly what they need. MedShare International of Atlanta has committed to sorting and cataloguing the supplies so they can be ordered on the Internet "warehouse." The supplies will be shipped in cargo containers with an estimated value of $400,000 per shipment.

Dr. Charash was inspired to create Doc to Dock by his participation in the first Clinton Global Initiative in 2005, and the first shipment went out a year later to Ghana. To date, Doc to Dock has collected $5 million worth of supplies and has commitments for $25 million more a year through the North Shore–Long Island Jewish Health System, a fifteen-hospital network. Plans are under way for twenty to thirty more containers to be sent to Libya over the next couple of years. The program's overhead works out to be about $20,000 per container filled with $400,000 worth of equipment and supplies, a return of twenty to one.

A few years ago Sheri Saltzberg and Mark Grashow of New York, recently retired from public health administration and teaching, went to Zambia for a wedding. Their son suggested they go to Zimbabwe to visit a family that had befriended him and to see Victoria Falls. While they were there, they visited several schools and were appalled to see that there were no textbooks, empty libraries, no science equipment, no basic school supplies, and often no school breakfast or lunch.

When they got home they founded their own NGO, the U.S.-Africa Children's Fellowship, and formed a partnership with the Zimbabwe Organization of Rural Associations for Progress, which had been working since 1980 to help improve the economy and education in individual communities.

Over the next two years, they located thirty-five U.S. schools to partner with thirty-five schools in Zimbabwe, and they've shipped four forty-foot containers to the schools, with more than 150,000 books, school supplies, toys, games, sports equipment, bicycles, clothing, sewing machines, agricultural tools, and other items. They raise funds for items needed but not donated—school uniforms, locally printed books, and educational materials and scholarships.

In the U.S. partner schools, Mark and Sheri try to give students an appreciation for what life is like for their counterparts in Zimbabwe. American kids learn that the kids in their partner school often get up at 5 a.m. to walk several miles to school, may well have nothing to eat, and may have lost one or both parents to AIDS. They also learn that many kids don't go to school at all because they can't afford the school fees, uniforms, or even a notebook and pencil; they have to work to support or stay home to care for a sick parent or younger sibling; or they don't have shoes and can't walk long distances in winter. The American children are empowered to take action—collecting donations and writing letters to the Zimbabwean students.

Mark and Sheri themselves fly to Zimbabwe as each shipment arrives and help distribute the donations to the schools. "The effects of the shipment have far exceeded anything we dreamed of," says Mark. "For the first time, students can take books home to read. Five percent of the kids in the seventh grade used to pass reading tests; now it's 60 percent. Three years ago, only one student in his district passed his A-level exams for university. This year, thirty-eight students passed. There are now art and sewing classes. Soccer flourishes because there's an abundance of soccer balls. Attendance in many kindergartens has increased three-fold due to the introduction of toys. In September we'll increase the schools we partner with from thirty-five to fifty." The program has proven so successful, there's now a waiting list of three hundred schools.

Why did they do this? Mark says, "I believe that each of us has an obligation to level the playing field of life. Schools that have no books, communities without water, and people without access to medical care are not someone else's problem. We all have a capacity to make a difference somewhere. We just have to decide if we have the will to do it."

John Wood made that decision after a trek to Nepal in 1998. A highly successful, overworked Microsoft executive, Wood went to Nepal to get away from the hectic pace of his old life. Instead, he found the driving passion of the rest of his life. On the first day of his twenty-one-day odyssey, Wood met a Nepalese education official who told him the children were eager to learn but had no books. He then took Wood to see a school with students who began learning English in first grade but whose library had so few books they were locked in a cabinet to keep them from being damaged. The headmaster told him, "Perhaps, sir, you will come back someday with books."

Wood came home, quit his job, and founded Room to Read, with the goal of providing education access to ten million children in the developing world. In 2000, he began working with rural communities to build schools and establish libraries with English and local language books, and posters, games, furniture, and flooring. In just six years, Room to Read has built 287 schools, established more than 3,600 libraries, donated almost 1.5 million English books, and published about that many local language books in 144 different titles. It has also set up 117 computer and language labs and funded more than 2,300 scholarships for girls in places where they otherwise would not go to school. Room to Read has expanded into several other Asian nations, begun work in South Africa in 2006, and plans to move into Latin America and more African nations by 2010.

John Wood has told his own story in *Leaving Microsoft to Change the World*, "an entrepreneur's odyssey to educate the world's children." Just think what would happen if a couple of hundred people followed his example and that of Sheri Saltzberg and Mark Grashow, or if a few thousand simply spent their next vacation working to put all the world's children in schools, with books and other learning materials. They could do it.

Another unique global giver is World Bicycle Relief. After the tsunami, World Bicycle Relief raised $1.5 million, in cooperation with the large Christian NGO World Vision International, to provide more than 24,000 bicycles to people in Sri Lanka. The bikes fill a wide variety of needs. A student still living in a transitional shelter who wants to be a teacher no longer has to take two bus rides each to and from school, and so has more time to study. A carpenter uses his bike to save time and money going to and from work. A fish seller and a fishnet maker use their bikes to take their kids to school and increase their business. A midwife's bicycle enables her to make twice as many home visits a day. The bicycles help to combat poverty in Sri Lanka another way too—they're manufactured locally, according to specific quality standards. World Bicycle Relief is now working on its next big project—providing 26,000 bicycles in six African countries, beginning with pilot programs for health-care workers and for people who want the bikes in order to pursue business opportunities. Again, there will be maximum use of local manufacturing, assembly, and supply chains.

In 2004, Procter & Gamble made a commitment to provide affordable safe drinking water to poor communities in developing countries, in which six thousand children die from contaminated water every day. Procter & Gamble has developed a valuable product, PUR Purifier of Water, which comes in a small packet sufficient to purify ten liters of water for consumption. Along with its partners Save the Children, UNICEF, the U.S. government foreign assistance program, and many others, Procter & Gamble has provided fifty million PUR packets on a not-for-profit basis, enough to purify 500 million liters of safe drinking water. The company has committed to provide packets to purify 35 million more liters to provide safe water to one million more African children in their schools, orphanages, and homes.

WHEN HURRICANE KATRINA devastated New Orleans, thousands of musicians lost their instruments. For many, that meant losing their livelihood as well. To replace the instruments, Gibson Guitar Corporation partnered with The Edge of U2, MusiCares, Conn-Selmer, VH1, MTV, and others to establish Music Rising. Gibson donated time and timber from Katrina states to make guitars, then produced a second set of Music Rising Guitars featuring The Edge's artwork. The money raised from selling the second set of guitars was used to help buy instruments for 2,200 Gulf Coast musicians. Music Rising has also helped rebuild music programs in churches and schools affecting an additional twenty thousand Gulf Coast residents.

The shortage of musical instruments in America goes far beyond the reach of Katrina's wreckage. Over the past several years, many schools have eliminated or sharply curtailed their instrumental music programs under budgetary pressures brought on by record enrollments, resistance to property-tax increases, and increased emphasis on and testing in reading and math. Ironically, the music cutbacks have undermined students' progress in other areas. Several scientific studies have demonstrated that children who learn to play a musical instrument have increased success in reading and math, improved self-esteem, better ability to work in teams, higher school-attendance rates, and a greater likelihood of graduating from high school and going on to college. For most kids, the public schools offer the only opportunity to learn to play an instrument, since their parents can't afford to buy them instruments or pay for lessons.

The VH1 Save the Music Foundation is determined to give the gift of music back to America's children, regardless of their financial situation. Sponsored by the popular music channel VH1 and its partners, Save the Music provides new instruments to school music programs in return for a school district's commitment to fund music teachers' salaries, necessary supplies, and maintenance, and to schedule music classes during the school day. Over the last decade, Save the Music has given more than $30 million worth of new instruments to more than one thousand public schools in eighty cities, helping more than 700,000 students know the joy of playing a horn, a string instrument, a keyboard, or a drum. The instruments are purchased locally, at discount rates.

At the urging of my friend John Sykes, then president of VH1, I got involved with Save the Music during my second term in the White House, donating a saxophone and attending events to publicize the effort. Although Save the Music only gives new instruments, most older horns can be restored to fine playing condition. I own a 1915 soprano saxophone, a 1935 Selmer tenor, a 1955 Buffet alto, and a tenor sax made by Adolph Sax himself in 1861. The only limitations on the music they can make are mine. So if you have an older horn you'll never play again, you should consider donating it to a school music program that needs it, after making sure it's in good working order. You might be changing a life.

Even if you can't make guitars or paint them, chances are you have things people need. Clothes you no longer want will be put to good use by Goodwill, the Salvation Army, or your local homeless shelter, which probably also needs new toothbrushes, toothpaste, combs, and shampoo. Coats, sweaters, and sweatshirts are important gifts when it gets cold. If you have business clothes you're willing to part with, you can leverage your donation by making it to Dress for Success, which supports economic independence for disadvantaged women, or its counterpart for men, Career Gear.

Dress for Success celebrates its tenth anniversary in 2007. It serves more than forty thousand women each year in the United States, Canada, the United Kingdom, and New Zealand. Women come to the program from homeless and domestic violence shelters, immigration services, educational institutions, and job-training programs. Each woman gets a suit, and accessories if they're available, appropriate for the industry for which she's interviewing. Once she finds a job, Dress for Success will supply additional clothing that can be mixed and matched. It also provides critical job-retention and career-development services, so you know that any clothing you contribute is likely to help someone become independent and successful.

Career Gear is a similar organization for low-income workingmen and men who want to get off public assistance. It works much like Dress for Success. A man gets one suit when he has an interview and another when he has a job, along with support for job retention. There is also an alumni program to help with budgeting, housing, nutrition, time and stress management, and job advancement. Career Gear accepts new and used suits, dress shirts, contemporary ties, and unworn shoes. They ask donors to give only clothing they would feel comfortable wearing to an interview, and they especially need big and tall sizes.

Another opportunity for giving is a sports program that serves kids whose families can't afford the necessary equipment or outfits. Because I'm an avid golfer, I'm especially partial to First Tee, which provides golf instruction for young people of all backgrounds. First Tee has gotten so big that golf club makers supply most of their needs, but they can still usually make good use of golf clubs and balls; in addition, many public golf courses run their own independent programs for kids who need clubs. If you provide them, chances are you'll be helping a boy or girl who'll soon be playing the game better than you do.

I've been supporting golf and clothing programs for a long time. Several times a year, I look over my clubs and clothes and if there are things I'm not using and that I'm not emotionally attached to, I send them where they will be of more benefit. Of course, because of the fortunate life I've had I accumulate too many clothes and good golf clubs, but lots of people have things incidental to their lives that would benefit others more.

One giving program I really like because people of all ages and income levels can participate is Operation Christmas Child, run by Samaritan's Purse, a Christian NGO led by Rev. Franklin Graham that is committed to following the example of the Good Samaritan by aiding the poor, sick, and suffering. Samaritan's Purse runs relief, community development, educational, vocational, and medical programs throughout the world. Operation Christmas Child began in the United Kingdom in 1990 to provide gifts to Romanian children. In 1993, Samaritan's Purse adopted it and solicited gifts that would fit in a shoebox, including small toys, hygiene products, and school supplies. Twenty-eight thousand boxes filled with gifts were delivered to Bosnian children in the first year. A couple of years later, I went to Bosnia and saw at first hand the happiness and gratitude sparked by those small boxes. Over the past fourteen years, Samaritan's Purse has collected and distributed more than fifty million boxes to boys and girls in more than 125 countries. In 2006 alone, about eight million boxes were delivered to ninety-five countries. Countless gift-givers of modest means have made a real difference in the lives of children who otherwise might have been forgotten. Though Samaritan's Purse is a Christian group, it offers a proven model of caring for children that members of any synagogue, mosque, or temple might want to emulate.

One of the most unusual examples of giving things I've come across is Locks of Love, which provides hairpieces to financially disadvantaged children under age eighteen suffering from hair loss from any medical condition. Most of the children the organization helps have lost their hair due to alopecia areata, a condition of uncertain cause and with no known cure. Locks of Love was started by Madonna Coffman, a retired cardiac nurse who developed alopecia in her twenties after a hepatitis vaccination. With the help of medication, she eventually recovered her hair, but fifteen years later, her four-year-old daughter developed the condition and lost all her hair. While she also recovered, her condition drove Madonna to take on Locks of Love full-time. She began with a garageful of donated hairpieces. Soon she secured office space from a hospital in Palm Beach, Florida, where she lived, and found a manufacturer of high-quality hair prostheses.

Locks of Love provides more than two hundred hairpieces a year to children in all fifty states and Canada. Hair is donated by thousands of people from all over America, often by children whose schools take it on as an annual project. Students at a school near my home in New York participate and have a good time doing it, in part because most of them have to grow their hair longer. The minimum hair length Locks of Love accepts is ten inches. If you can grow your hair that long, you can provide a great gift to a deserving child.

Another giving project that could be replicated in every community is the Backpack Club. Despite all the government programs designed to prevent hunger among low-income people, including food stamps, school lunches, and nutrition aid to women and young children, many families with children don't have enough money to buy groceries and pay their bills. In 2004, the U.S. Department of Agriculture said that almost 12 percent of American households—13.5 million—were unsure of their ability to feed themselves at some point during the year, and about a third of them said at least one family member went hungry at least some of the time. Only 12 percent of the hungry are homeless; 93 percent are citizens; nearly half live in rural or suburban areas; and more than one-third have at least one working adult, often working nights and weekends. Until 2007, we hadn't raised the minimum wage in a decade. Many of these people just don't have enough money to pay the rent and utilities, buy gas, and feed their kids, especially if a medical emergency arises.

There are hundreds of local food banks in America that collect food and give it to needy families, often to children at schools who take it home. In 1995, the Arkansas Rice Depot determined that some kids at the Martin Luther King Elementary School in Little Rock were reluctant to take the food, despite their hunger, because they were being teased for being poor. To solve the problem, the depot put the food in backpacks, which could also be filled with books and school supplies.

That's how the Backpack Club movement started. Today there are at least seventy food banks distributing tens of thousands of backpacks full of food every week, at a cost of $2 to $3, and a weight of seven to ten pounds. The food banks have to raise the money locally for the backpacks and child-specific food. If your community has a Backpack Club, you can support a family for $2 to $3 a week, or work with a participating congregation or civic club to do more. If you don't have one, you could probably find more than enough support to start a Backpack Club once your neighbors learn about the need and relatively low cost of meeting it. This is one area that ought to be covered by closing the gaps in government support programs, but that hasn't happened. Serving all those kids going home with their backpacks to get themselves and their families through the weekend is a big reward for stepping into the breach.

WHAT IF YOU WANT to give something useful that you don't presently own or you have things of value but they have no evident charitable use? Laina Niemi, an American who followed the 2006 Clinton Global Initiative on the

Internet, found a good answer to the first question. She committed to buying and donating oral rehydration solution packets to UNICEF to reduce diarrhea-induced death among children in developing countries. The packets cost only 6 cents each.

For people who want to give things away that have value but no charitable purpose, eBay Giving Works has provided a unique solution. You can sell the items on eBay and donate part or all of the final sale price to your chosen nonprofit organization; eBay collects and distributes the donations to the charities and issues tax receipts to the seller. You can also give in-kind contributions to one of the more than ten thousand NGOs fund-raising on eBay, and they can sell them in an eBay store. Either way, the process turns a gift of anything of value into useful support of any good endeavor.

More than five thousand in-kind contributions to the Points of Light Foundation have generated more than $600,000 in revenues. The Prostate Cancer Foundation raised more than $200,000 from the sale of 350 items. The Red Cross in Washington State has generated almost $700,000 from the sale of 3,500 items over the past three years. The House Ear Institute brought in $59,000 to support hearing-health research from the sale of 244 items. The Laura Iverson Gallery sells original oil paintings on eBay to raise funds for a variety of charities. This kind of giving is bound to increase in the future. Buyers and sellers by the millions meet on eBay's marketplace. If just a small fraction were part of eBay's Giving Works, the givers of things would drastically increase the capacity of thousands of good organizations to pursue their missions.

One final note on giving things. We all want to give useful things to victims of natural disasters like Hurricane Katrina or the tsunami, but giving usefully in the immediate aftermath of an emergency can be difficult, because even though clothes, toiletries, bedding, food, and toys are needed, there are likely to be bottlenecks in the transportation or distribution networks. To avoid them, you have to be careful in your giving. For example, shortly after the tsunami hit South Asia, Hillary and I visited the New York Buddhist Vihara Temple in Queens to support its efforts to collect supplies to send to Sri Lanka. Their neighbors of all faiths were so eager to help that the Buddhists were able to fill a moving van with large cardboard boxes. Of course the van could not drive to Sri Lanka, so the temple asked Hillary to help them find a cargo container to ship the goods to Sri Lanka, where members of another temple would see to their distribution. They got their container and their Sri Lankan counterparts received and delivered the goods. Meanwhile, other groups were sending donated goods by air in such volume that there was a huge backlog of crates on the tarmac at the Colombo airport, leading to some significant spoilage and lack of delivery. This cautionary tale doesn't mean you shouldn't give things in an emergency, but it does demonstrate why unless you know that your gift will reach its destination in time, it's often better in such circumstances to send even a modest financial contribution to an established charity or relief organization used to dealing with the unique logistical problems that large numbers of needy people in a disaster present.

FIVE

Giving Skills

——

ONE OF THE greatest gifts anyone can give is a useful skill. Most of us know how to do something not everyone can do as well as we can. Transferring that knowledge and the ability to use it can empower others in amazing ways.

Perhaps the most common volunteer skills-giver in the United States is the reading tutor. Every week, thousands of Americans tutor young people and immigrants who want to learn English. When I was president, we increased the number of tutors dramatically through a partnership with colleges and universities called America Reads. Participating schools allowed their students to earn federal work-study funds, not by doing jobs on campus but by going into community schools to help young children improve their reading skills, a precondition to success in all other subjects.

Tutoring is a great way of giving that's open to volunteers in almost every community, but as with other kinds of giving, it's not always easy to do well. Sometimes even very literate volunteers don't know everything necessary to teach or to monitor the progress of those they're committed to help. In 2001, Gary Kosman founded an organization called America Learns to provide guidance and support to tutors and mentors, and to help them improve, evaluate, and report on the performance of their students in the least costly and time-consuming ways available. Kosman got the idea for America Learns from his own experience as a reading tutor. Several years ago, he couldn't help a student who was supposed to underline all the predicates in her reading material. He had forgotten what a predicate is and couldn't find out from a quick search. If you're interested in being a reading tutor but have forgotten some of the basics, the America Learns network can help you and other tutors with whom you serve. America Learns, like America Reads and all other tutoring programs, is a skills-giver, enabling anyone who can read well and has an hour or two a week to volunteer to do so with the confidence that he or she can really help.

Another skills-giving program I learned about more than twenty years ago helps children well before they start school, when their brains, emotions, and outlooks are rapidly developing. Especially in those preschool years, parents are their children's most important teachers. Almost all of them want to do a good job, but for a variety of reasons many lack the skills to do so. That's where HIPPY comes in.

Home Instruction for Parents of Preschool Youngsters was developed in Israel in 1969 by Dr. Avima Lombard to help new immigrants prepare their young children to succeed in school. HIPPY empowers parents as their children's first teachers by giving them the tools, skills, and confidence to work with their children at home. A typical HIPPY site reaches up to 180 children and their parents with one coordinator and twelve to eighteen part-time home visitors. The program is open to any parent, but is designed to help those families coping with poverty, lack of education, and social isolation.

In 1986, Hillary persuaded Dr. Lombard to help her establish a HIPPY program in Arkansas. She described the HIPPY formula for success in her book *It Takes a Village:*

> A staff member recruited from the community comes into the home once a week and role-plays with the parent (usually the mother), demonstrating for her how she can work with her child to stimulate cognitive development. Along with special activity packets, the program employs common household objects to illustrate concepts. For example, a spoon and a fork might be used to demonstrate differences in shape or sharpness, or the volume control on the TV might be tuned up and down to teach concepts of loud and soft. The material in the activity packets, designed for parents who may not read well themselves, is outlined in straightforward fifteen-minute daily lesson plans arranged in a developmental sequence. The usual starting age is four, and most children participate for two years. Some programs add a third year, so children can begin the program at the age of three.
>
> When we brought HIPPY into rural areas and housing projects in Arkansas, a number of educators and others did not believe that parents who had not finished high school were up to the task of teaching their children. Many of the parents doubted their own abilities. One mother whose home I visited told me she had always known she was supposed to put food on the table and a roof over her children's heads, but no one had ever told her before that she was supposed to be her son's first teacher.
>
> Not only did the program help kids get jump-

started in the right direction; it also gave the parents a boost in self-confidence. Many of them became interested in learning for themselves as well as for their children, going back to school to get a high school equivalency degree or even starting college. This is a particularly important development, because researchers cite a mother's level of education as one of the key factors in determining whether her children do well in school. It stands to reason that when a mother furthers her own learning, she becomes more engaged in her child's.

In 1988, HIPPY USA was established as an independent NGO headquartered in New York City. There are now about 146 HIPPY programs in twenty-five states and the District of Columbia, serving more than sixteen thousand children and their families. HIPPY has also expanded to Australia, New Zealand, Canada, Germany, and South Africa. I wish there were HIPPY programs in every community with a significant number of single mothers or poor, uneducated parents. Anyone who has ever been to a HIPPY graduation ceremony and seen the pride and self-confidence of both the parents and children would agree. Even if you are not the parent of a school-aged child, you can take the lead in bringing HIPPY to your town, volunteer to be a home visitor, or support them with money or other services.

MANY PROMINENT SPORTS figures have foundations that support young people through educational and scholarship programs. The most innovative ones I've seen in terms of skills development are the Andre Agassi College Preparatory Academy and the Tiger Woods Learning Center.

Agassi Prep is a public charter school located in the Las

Vegas neighborhood with the city's highest percentage of at-risk kids. A charter school, while part of the public system, is free to experiment with innovative teaching and learning methods that may or may not be consistent with school district guidelines. There are a few thousand of these schools in the United States, started by teachers, parents, entrepreneurs, retired military officers, and others. School districts are supposed to judge charter schools on results, extending the charter if children show improved educational performance, revoking it if they don't. By that measure, the school funded by Andre Agassi's foundation should be around for a long time.

Ninety-eight percent of Agassi Prep's students are minority, most from low-income families. Many students came to the school testing one or two years behind their grade level. In Clark County, where Las Vegas is located, more than half the schools failed to make "adequate yearly progress" according to Department of Education benchmarks. Agassi Prep has cleared the "adequate progress" bar every year since its inception. In 2005, its middle school was the only school in the county to receive the top-level "exemplary" designation. In recent testing, students in some grades exhibited more than a year's academic advancement in several subjects in less than four months.

How do they do it? Class size is capped at nineteen students for kindergarten, twenty-one for first grade, and twenty-five for other grades. The school day is two hours longer and the school year is ten days longer than in regular public schools. Students spend one-third more "time on task" than in a traditional public school. Even after the longer school day, 85 percent of the students voluntarily stay another one or two hours for tutoring, elective courses, or extracurricular activities. Teachers, parents, and students sign a compact of commitment to their respective roles, and students recite a "Code of Respect" that reflects the school's special rules. Teachers and administrators are on yearly contracts with no tenure, but get bonuses for meeting or exceeding performance standards. Within the campus, there are several modern computer labs, two computer and touch screen SMART Boards in every classroom, and laptops that high school students can use anywhere on campus. Parents are encouraged to visit and to make use of the school's computers after classes are over. The school is developing an internship program with local businesses and a college credit program that will provide high school students a chance to secure credits equal to one year of college by the time they graduate.

These "best practices" are producing extremely positive results. A few are contingent on the generous support Agassi provides, but most could be adopted in any charter school with the backing of parents, teachers, and an effective, committed principal. The Frederick Douglass Academy is a public school within a mile of my office in Harlem. Its student body is 97 percent African American and Hispanic, has a 93 percent graduation rate, scores above the citywide average on the state Regents Exam, and has an 87 percent college-going rate, 20 percent higher than the city average. It can be done.

I've visited Agassi Prep and talked to Andre several times about his passion for it. When I asked him how creating the school compared with winning a tennis tournament, he said, "Tennis was a stepping-stone for me. It gave me the chance to do this. Changing a child's life is what I always wanted to do. Winning a tennis tournament doesn't compare to the anticipation of what these kids will do with their lives."

The Tiger Woods Learning Center is located on four-

teen acres in Anaheim, California. Of course it has a beautifully landscaped golf driving range and practice grounds, but
the real action goes on inside the 35,000-square-foot educational facility. After school and on weekends, young people
have a chance to go beyond their normal classroom work
with unique enrichment programs that include forensic science, engineering, aerospace, video production, and home
design. In February 2006, on my tour of the facility, I
observed students solving medical problems, operating
robots they built themselves, and learning from model
spaceships they were constructing. The mission of the
Woods Center is to provide students a broader perspective
of the world, an appreciation of their own skills, and the
tools to achieve long-term success. The students I saw
clearly understood what they were doing and were able to
explain their experiments in a direct, concise manner.

Tiger Woods knows most kids can't grow up to be the
world's greatest golfer, but they have big dreams, and he's
giving them a chance to follow them. His center relies on
well-trained teachers and dedicated mentors. If you live in
Southern California and have a background in one of the
center's areas of concentration, you might want to become a
mentor. If you live somewhere else, you might want to join
with others to find one or more benefactors to finance a similar operation, offer to volunteer, and give kids the same
kinds of opportunities. It could open up a new world for the
students and brighten the future of all Americans.

America is facing a shortage of young people going into
math, science, and advanced technology. If young women
and African-American and Hispanic men were to enter these
fields at the same rate as Caucasian and Asian males, the
shortage would be dramatically reduced or eliminated alto-
gether. The Woods Center has demonstrated one way to

help that happen. Its students are girls and boys, African American, Hispanic, and Caucasian, from East and South Asia and the Middle East.

Another citizen-led effort to address the shortage of engineers and engineering technicians deserves mention. In 2007, the National Academy Foundation is launching a four-year effort to establish 110 Academies of Engineering in urban school districts across the United States designed to produce 8,800 high school graduates a year who will go on to college and careers in engineering and engineering technology. The project will emphasize increased participation of women and underrepresented minorities, preparing them for post-secondary studies by ensuring their competence in required mathematics, science, and technical subjects.

Over the next decade, employment demand in all engineering fields is projected to increase by more than 13 percent, with demand for engineering technicians increasing by nearly 12 percent. In 2005 women made up almost half the U.S. workforce, but only 10 percent of all engineers were female. African Americans comprised 10.8 percent of the workforce but only 3 percent of the engineers. The comparable figures for Hispanics were 13 percent and 4 percent.

If any NGO can make a dent in this problem, it's the National Academy Foundation. Founded in 1980 by Sandy Weill, chairman emeritus of Citigroup, NAF, in partnership with local business leaders, forms small, career-themed learning communities in large urban high schools. Its established academies in finance, information technology, and hospitality and tourism prepare students for college and introduce them to the world of work with the help of adult mentors and advisors. For an annual cost of $260 per student, NAF runs 529 academies supporting the development of more than fifty thousand students, 70 percent of whom are minorities. NAF students have a high school graduation rate of 90 percent, 23 percent higher than the overall graduation rate in the high schools in which the academy operates. More than 80 percent go on to college. Fifty-two percent complete their degrees in four years, compared to the national average of 32 percent, and they are 60 percent less likely than all students to require remedial coursework when they begin college.

NAF works in part because of the involvement of two thousand companies and thousands of mentors. If you or your business is interested in participating, your time will be well spent. The NAF model works. We just need more young people involved in it.

BOTH YOUNG PEOPLE and adults need basic knowledge about how our economy functions as well as the skills to make it work for them. Operation HOPE seeks to give those skills to people who otherwise would be left out and left behind. Founded by John Hope Bryant in May 1992 in the immediate aftermath of the Los Angeles riots, Operation HOPE has set an ambitious objective: to launch a "silver rights" movement in America. The movement's agenda includes teaching financial literacy to "low-wealth" children; promoting inner-city communities to investors and lenders; empowering adults with skills in money management, credit, mortgage, business lending, and small-business operations; increasing home and small-business ownership; teaching inner-city residents computer literacy in its Cyber Café; and through its HOPE Centers, converting lower-income check cashers into banking customers, renters into homeowners, minimum-wage workers into living-wage earners, small-business hopefuls into business owners, and the economically uneducated into the financially literate.

Since its inception, Operation HOPE has attracted more than $100 million in grant funds and about $300 million in mortgages and small-business loans. It has formed partnerships with three hundred private companies, more than one hundred government agencies, and more than one thousand NGOs. Operating in more than seven hundred schools and community-based organizations across the United States, HOPE has educated more than 200,000 low-wealth young people in financial literacy. I participated in one of Bryant's Banking on Our Future financial-literacy classes in Harlem and saw firsthand how eager young people are to learn. It was fascinating to watch John demonstrate, in easily understandable terms, what a check is and how to write one, even on the sleeve of a shirt!

After Katrina hit the Gulf Coast, Operation HOPE joined my foundation and ACORN, an NGO of grassroots activists committed to empowering poor people, to assist eligible survivors to claim the earned income tax credit. Together, HOPE and ACORN helped people secure more than $10 million to which they were entitled but for which they had to apply. Operation HOPE also provided free tax counseling and aid with the special problems faced by people who had lost their homes and their jobs. And H&R Block gave free assistance in tax preparation and EITC filing to five thousand HOPE clients.

John Bryant is a forty-one-year-old whirlwind of ideas and action. Lean, intense, focused, and completely positive in his belief in the potential of poor people to prosper with "a hand up not a hand out," Bryant has attracted support from Democrats and Republicans alike. President George W. Bush appointed him to the board for the Community Development Financial Institutions Fund, and he has worked with my foundation and hundreds of other partners to advance his goals.

When I asked Bryant why he decided to devote his life to Operation HOPE, he said, "I don't know if I decided. In 1992 I was twenty-six and financially successful, but I wasn't happy. When the Los Angeles riots broke out after Rodney King was beaten, I was appalled by the indifference to the plight of people without hope. I wanted to change hearts and minds, to teach poor people to live with hope and to persuade people with money to invest in them, in their children, homes, and business—not out of charity but enlightened self-interest. I started Operation HOPE out of guilt, pain, and a need to heal myself. I keep doing it because the key to happiness is to stop focusing on me and start focusing on we. My family still has everything we need, and I feel lucky that I made my decision at twenty-six instead of waiting until I was seventy."

A large portion of Operation HOPE's success is due to citizen volunteers. Bryant calls them HOPE Heroes. They provide financial literacy education to young people, financial counseling to disaster victims, and economic education in credit, investment, and homeownership to adults. If you have the necessary skills, Operation HOPE can use you.

In almost every community of any size there is a Boys and Girls Club or a Girls Inc. chapter. They depend on local volunteers to support full-time staff in providing a range of skills from tutoring to teamwork to personal and leadership development to community service. In late 2006, I spoke at the annual fund-raising luncheon of the local Girls Inc. chapter in Omaha, Nebraska. More than three thousand people came to support the amazing work the staff and volunteers are doing to help girls and young women overcome obstacles to their success, through a range of after-school, weekend, and summer activities offered at Girls Inc. centers, schools, churches, community centers, and housing projects.

I was introduced by a six-year veteran of Girls Inc, a sixteen-year-old African American, Symone Sanders. Her involvement with the program has included a trip to Washington, D.C., helping to film and edit promotional videos for the organization, participating in her club's media literacy program, and serving as a student representative on the Girls Inc. board of trustees. Symone wants to go to law school and become a judge. She's come a long way and is going a lot further. There are many kids like her whose lives could be launched by caring adults. Volunteering at Girls Inc. or Boys and Girls Clubs offers you the chance to be one of them.

One skill we often mistakenly assume people already have is the ability to take good care of themselves through proper eating, exercise, and sleep. The percentage of overweight Americans has increased dramatically in the last twenty years, as we eat more and exercise and sleep less. Too many people's habits are determined by consideration of convenience and immediate cost, and too few children learn how to live healthy lifestyles at home or in school. The United States, United Kingdom, Ireland, and other nations are waging national campaigns against childhood obesity, the alarming rise in diabetes, and other health problems that undermine our physical, psychological, and economic well-being. Governments, schools, and large organizations are becoming more involved, but there is still plenty of room and need for citizen action. Danny Abraham is a fitness fanatic who made his fortune in the diet product Slim-Fast. When the Mayo Clinic cured him of a serious lung infection, he realized that many of the employees who were caring for others were not in the best shape themselves, so he built them two health-club facilities. One thousand Mayo employees, medical students, retirees, volunteers, and spouses visit them every day. Of course most people can't give that much to others, but there's a lot anyone can do. You can work to improve your local school's meals and expand its physical education program; to promote exercise programs at senior citizen centers; to educate people with low incomes and busy schedules on how to buy and prepare healthy foods; to lobby local governments for more open space in which people can walk, jog, bike, and play; and much more. Trainers at local health spas can volunteer to go into schools to teach kids that exercise is fun and you're never too out of shape to start. They can also help people with disabilities use their bodies to the maximum of their potential.

Skills-giving is going on in every region in the world, and there are many valuable projects under way that should be expanded or adopted by others. Here are a few that I've been exposed to.

In the Middle East, much of the rapidly growing youth population is frustrated by the absence of economic opportunity and by being cut off from the positive aspects of global interdependence. The senseless waste of their talent and potential makes them more vulnerable to the nihilist ideas of extremists, at the very least perpetuating a culture of resentment and powerlessness. Young Arab Leaders is a network of young men and women committed to making the opportunities of the global economy available to more young people throughout the Arab world. Established in 2004, YAL already has chapters in eleven Arab nations and plans to be active in the rest of them by 2008. The group's mission is to spread leadership values and help develop future leaders with a positive vision; contribute to the region's development with results-driven initiatives that address its most important challenges; and assist in bridging the "awareness gap" between Arabs and the rest of the world.

I met with the group in Dubai just as they were getting started and have met with them several times since. YAL now has more than five hundred members from diverse backgrounds, including business, politics, media, academia, the arts, science, and civil society. They represent the "other" Arab world we hear too little about in the mass media, because they are builders, not destroyers.

Young Arab Leaders participated in the Clinton Global Initiative in 2005 and 2006, and made important skills-giving commitments. They launched an Entrepreneurship Initiative, a competition to review thousands of business plans, identify two hundred for further review, then select thirty to be developed into concrete business projects with the financial backing of YAL business "angels," already successful Arab business and financial enterprises. The group also committed to partner with Business for Diplomatic Action to recruit young YAL members for internships with top U.S. companies, vowing to "out-recruit bin Laden." YAL is also working to improve Arab education systems to meet modern job-market needs, and organizing dialogues between young Arabs and their counterparts from other parts of the world. If Young Arab Leaders succeeds in its efforts, Arab societies will offer more equal and constructive life choices for young women and men, and all our children will live in a more peaceful, prosperous, cooperative world.

Women for Women International teaches skills to one of the world's most disadvantaged groups: women in war-torn regions. Ninety percent of those killed or injured in modern conflicts are civilians, many of them women and children. The women who survive are forced to bear terrible burdens as the sole breadwinners and caregivers for children and elderly parents. They have often suffered rape, torture, starvation, and forced prostitution in ruined economies filled with unresolved animosities, and they rarely have the access men do to educational, political, and financial resources.

Since its founding in 1993, Women for Women International has taken 93,000 women "on a journey from victim to survivor to active citizen," providing skills in job training, running a small business, and political activism. It has also distributed more than $30 million in direct aid and microcredit loans. In Afghanistan it registered thousands of women to vote in the presidential election. In Nigeria it helped women organize themselves to end female genital mutilation and oppressive widowhood practices. In Rwanda, women have been trained to prevent malaria. In Bosnia, its microcredit and skills-training efforts have helped nearly ten thousand women, who have a 98 percent loan repayment rate.

Women for Women was founded by Zainab Salbi and her husband, Amjad Atallah. Salabi escaped a difficult and dangerous life in Saddam Hussein's Iraq and wrote *Between Two Worlds: Escape from Tyranny: Growing Up in the Shadow of Saddam*, a powerful memoir about her experience. In response to the fate of women in rape camps in Bosnia, they created one-on-one "sister-to-sister" connections between sponsors in the United States and survivors. This year, Women for Women will serve more than thirty thousand women in Afghanistan, Iraq, Colombia, Bosnia, Kosovo, Nigeria, Rwanda, the Democratic Republic of Congo, and Sudan. Each woman has a sponsor, who provides direct financial assistance for one year and exchanges letters with her "sister." The sponsors come from all fifty states and fifty-five other nations. They contribute just $27 per month, but in the affected countries that is enough for food, clean water, medicine, schoolbooks, and perhaps seed money for a small-business venture. Women for Women has helped its sisters make durable market baskets in Rwanda; raise and sell fish in Colombia; cultivate and sell flowers in Kosovo; and form a baking cooperative in Afghanistan.

Women for Women International's one-on-one model could expand almost indefinitely, given the number of women who need its help. To do so, it needs more sponsors and volunteers.

Not all skills-givers are wealthy or part of large organizations. Diane Stevens owns a beauty salon in Greenbelt, Maryland. She felt compassion for the people of Sierra Leone, who suffered through a decade-long civil war in the 1990s in which rebel forces, in their bloodlust for victory and control of the vast store of "blood diamonds," regularly cut off the arms and legs of noncombatant civilians, including children. When Diane learned that one of the victims was a hairdresser who worked all day standing on one leg, she decided she had to do something to help. She recruited three other stylists from her shop, along with three members of her church, to go on an eight-day trip to Sierra Leone, with expenses paid by her clients and their local government. Diane and her stylists will teach three hundred women in the capital city of Freetown about hair treatments, manicures, pedicures, and other techniques. She learned that Sierra Leoneans pride themselves on their appearance, especially their hair, and believes her cosmetology program can help alleviate the severe unemployment problem and raise morale. Think of all the good that could be done if other Americans with universally marketable skills followed her example in troubled countries half a world away, or troubled neighborhoods nearby.

Carlos Slim's life is very different from that of Diane Stevens, but he too is a deeply committed skills-giver. One of the world's wealthiest men, Slim owns Telmex, the Mexican telephone company, and a host of other business ventures. He is also an avid sports fan with an encyclopedic knowledge of sports history and current developments. The first time I met him, he was carrying a notebook in which he had written his list of the twentieth century's greatest athletes, his ranking of the twenty greatest baseball pitchers of all time, and his graphs of improvements in performance in various sports over the past hundred years. Currently, he is overseeing a major reconstruction and restoration effort in his hometown, Mexico City. And he is obsessed with Mexico's future and with giving more young Mexicans a chance to be a part of it.

His two foundations, Carso and Telmex, have combined assets in excess of $5 billion, and he plans to add another $5 billion by 2010. Over the last decade, they have paid for nearly 200,000 surgeries performed outside Mexico's main cities, financed more than 3,600 organ transplants, provided specialized equipment for about 2,400 newborns, supported cultural programs in 1,300 public and private institutions, and posted bail for 52,000 poor people.

These are remarkable achievements, but Slim's commitment to skills-giving will have an even larger impact on Mexico's future. Every year, Telmex Foundation provides computers for two thousand schools, bicycles for ten thousand children in rural areas to ride to school, and university scholarships for fifteen thousand students. In the last decade, Slim has sent a staggering 165,000 students to college. Every year, he brings ten thousand of his best scholarship students to Mexico City for a "Mexico in the 21st Century" day to hear from well-known political, social, and cultural figures, including Mikhail Gorbachev, former president of Spain Felipe González, Madeleine Albright, Lance Armstrong, Pelé, Magic Johnson, and Alvin Toffler. When I spoke there a couple of years ago, Carlos asked me to talk about big global issues, not about Mexico. He believes if young Mexicans understand the world beyond their borders, they will make better decisions about Mexico's future.

I began and now end this chapter on giving skills with education, because in the twenty-first century, education is the ultimate skills gift. While few people can give as much as Carlos Slim, almost everyone can be a reading tutor, or mentor a young person trying to decide what path to take in life, or give a bike to a schoolchild in a poor rural village, or contribute something to giving low-income kids at home and abroad the chance to go to college. Remember Oseola McCarty, whose story is told in chapter 2. Almost everyone who reads this book has a higher income than she had. If she can give so much, all of us can give something.

SIX

Gifts of Reconciliation
and New Beginnings

———

S INCE THE END of the Cold War, most of the world's
political violence within and between nations has
involved people of different religious, ethnic, and
tribal groups. While there are always underlying grievances
of varying degrees of legitimacy, political leaders have
exploited them to harden group identities and demonize,
even dehumanize, the "others," in order to increase popular
support in their struggle for power, land, or resources.
Regardless of the root causes, once violence driven by group
hatred begins, the vast majority of the victims are civilians,
often women and children. They have been subject to military assaults, suicide bombings, rape, dismemberment, torture, starvation, and mass slaughter.

In the aftermath, even the most open-minded people find
it difficult not to become hard-hearted. Yet in the Balkans,
Northern Ireland, the Middle East, Rwanda, or any other
place torn apart by group violence, the ability to see the
"others" as people—to respect them, communicate with
them, work with them, live alongside them, and yes, forgive

them—is essential to putting broken communities back together and moving on with life.

Of course, the most revered example of reconciling leadership is Nelson Mandela, who invited the men who guarded him in jail to his inauguration as president of South Africa, put leaders who had supported apartheid in his cabinet, and set up the Truth and Reconciliation Commission to give people who had committed crimes during the apartheid era the chance to avoid imprisonment by confessing. Mandela decided that the only way he or the people of South Africa could be free to face the future was to let go of the past. Because of all that he had suffered, he had the credibility to do it.

There are many other good and visionary men and women who are working to promote understanding, reconciliation, and new beginnings across great divides. I wish I could chronicle them all. This chapter tells the story of a few, how you can learn about others, and how you can get involved in this kind of giving.

In September 1993, when the historic Israeli-Palestinian peace accord was signed on the White House lawn, among the invited guests were a group of remarkable Jewish and Muslim teenagers from the Middle East. They were members of the first class of Seeds of Peace, a group founded earlier that year by the late author and journalist John Wallach, after the first attack on the World Trade Center. The first group included forty-six Israeli, Palestinian, and Egyptian teenagers. They met at a camp in Maine where they lived together, shared meals, and participated in athletic and arts activities. Most important, they had daily sessions in which they expressed their thoughts and feelings on the conflict back home and listened to others do the same.

Since that first summer, Seeds of Peace has grown ten-fold, with more than 450 teens from trouble spots around the world participating each summer. There are equal numbers of boys and girls. The Middle East delegation has been expanded to include students from Jordan, Morocco, Qatar, Yemen, and Tunisia. There are also American Seeds now, along with Turks, Greeks, Greek Cypriots and Turkish Cypriots; Indians, Pakistanis, and Afghans; and from the Balkans, Bosnians, Croatians, Serbs, Kosovars, and Macedonians. In 2004, Seeds included teams from Iraq, Saudi Arabia, and Kuwait in its Beyond Borders exchange program. Since 1993, more than three thousand young people from twenty-five nations have graduated from Seeds of Peace with a deeper commitment to understanding and reconciliation, and to sharing their experiences with their peers.

In addition to maintaining its camp in Maine, the organization has opened the Seeds of Peace Center for Coexistence in Jerusalem and launched an Advanced Coexistence Program in which two hundred Israelis and Palestinians meet in different locations on both sides of Jerusalem and throughout the West Bank and Israel.

These young people have done some amazing things together. In 1998, they met in Switzerland and actually developed their own Middle East Peace Plan, which resolved all outstanding issues, including the status of Jerusalem, the borders, and refugees. Seeds members have produced award-winning documentary films and instituted programs for younger Arab and Jewish children, and for refugees. They visit the White House and other important sites in Washington each year. When they reach college age, the organization offers them counseling on gaining admission to schools and financial assistance to help them pay for it when they do.

But the most important part of Seeds of Peace remains

the sustained human contact among young people of different religious and ethnic groups long at odds with each other. In its 2005 annual report, Shai, an Israeli girl, offered this testimony: "We have been given a new life at this camp. We must take it home and keep it alive, spreading its meaning wherever we go." Sabreen, a Palestinian said: "We—the teenagers—in Seeds of Peace can make a change in our families, communities, schools. It will be hard, but we can make it because we succeeded in doing that to ourselves." Mohammed, a Pakistani, declared, "We are warriors of hope, we are masters of understanding, we are pioneers of respect, we are soldiers of trust."

In 2000, in a heated phase of the Second Intifada, a seventeen-year-old very active Arab-Israeli Seeds of Peace member, Asel Asleh, was caught in a crossfire and killed while trying to help an injured friend. He had thirty Seeds of Peace T-shirts. He was buried in one of them. Anyone who supports Seeds of Peace is keeping that young man's legacy alive and giving all the world's children a better chance for a safer, brighter future.

PeacePlayers International is a youth-reconciliation program that brings people together around basketball. Founded in 2001, the organization, based in Washington, D.C., uses basketball to teach communication, cooperation, and teamwork through full-time programs in the Middle East, Northern Ireland, Cyprus, and South Africa. Over the last couple of years, PeacePlayers has been particularly active in the Middle East, sponsoring tournaments and camps, building basketball courts in the West Bank, and in February 2006, holding the first annual Desert Hoop Classic in Jericho, involving 150 coaches and kids from Jewish and Arab communities. Twice a week, the group also brings together "twin" schools for younger Arab and Jewish boys, ages ten to twelve, for basketball and sessions on coexistence and cooperation led by young adults from the communities.

So far, PeacePlayers has used basketball to help more than 35,000 young people get to know each other, develop leadership skills, and bridge divides in their home communities. The organization is now expanding its efforts in the Middle East by recruiting hundreds of young men and women, ages eighteen to twenty-two, to serve as coaches and mentors to thousands more young basketball players. They are selecting and training program directors from the United States, Israel, and the Palestinian territories to develop local mentors. Besides volunteers, each program has a full-time director, which costs $25,000 a year. Peace Players has been very successful and could greatly increase its efforts in the Middle East and elsewhere, but it needs more support to do so.

The Interfaith Youth Core is unique in its efforts to bring young people of diverse religions together to better understand each other's faiths and their own as testaments of peace that can prevent group hatred and violence before they arise. Founded by Dr. Eboo Patel, a thirty-one-year-old Indian-American Muslim from Chicago, the Interfaith Youth Core seeks not to dilute but to strengthen and deepen young people's religious convictions while helping them gain greater knowledge of the beliefs of others, identify values they have in common, and express those values through cooperation in community-service projects. Before the service work begins, the Core gives young people the opportunity to discuss with others how the scriptures, stories, rituals, and heroes of their respective faiths lead them to serve. Every year in April, the Core sponsors Days of Interfaith Youth Service in which young people come together on college campuses and in their hometowns to do community service and engage in dialogue. In 2006, more than fifty cities around the world participated.

Over the course of seven years, 10,300 young people on five continents have participated in Interfaith Youth Core programs. Since 2003, the Core has trained 770 organizers to develop and lead their own independent service programs, which have involved thousands of others around the world. If the old adage about an ounce of prevention being worth a pound of cure is correct, the Interfaith Youth Core is a good place to start.

Women play a unique role in most reconciliation efforts and in dealing with other problems that require new beginnings, like trafficking in women and girls, human rights abuses, and the use of children as soldiers. Indeed, a persuasive case can be made that if women were equal participants in every aspect of a nation's life, many of these problems would not occur in the first place.

In 1997, following up on her assertion two years earlier, at the Fourth U.N. Conference on Women in Beijing, that "women's rights are human rights," Hillary and Secretary of State Madeleine Albright established the Vital Voices Democracy Initiative to promote the advancement of women's rights as an explicit goal of U.S. foreign policy. Over the next three years, at conferences throughout the world, Vital Voices brought together thousands of women leaders from eighty countries. They included Catholic and Protestant women working together for peace in Northern Ireland; Muslim, Croatian, and Serbian women committed to peace in Bosnia; and African women lobbying to end female genital mutilation in their countries. In 2000, American women who were involved in the government initiative and who wanted the project to continue formed a new nongovernmental organization, Vital Voices Global Partnership, and aligned with other women around the world who began their own chapters.

Vital Voices invests in emerging women leaders to give them the tools they need to advance peace and reconciliation, run successful businesses, participate fully in their nation's political life, and combat trafficking in women and girls and other abusive practices. Vital Voices began working with women in Afghanistan, where the Taliban was particularly repressive to women and girls. With the Taliban shackles thrown off, the group is supporting Afghan women's right to full participation in the country's reconstruction, preparing them to be active in politics, civil society, and income-generating activities, and in making sure that Afghan girls have access to education and the opportunity to work in a field of their own choosing.

Vital Voices is also working with women in several African nations, across Asia, and in Russia and Ukraine. It combats human trafficking, in partnership with the U.S. government, corporations, NGOs, academic institutions such as New York University, and philanthropists like Alice Kandell. It is striving to increase the role of Muslim women in the Middle East and North Africa and in the economic and political life of their countries. It has partnered with Queen Rania and the Jordan River Foundation to enhance the status of women in Jordan. It has programs to advance the economic and human rights of women in Venezuela, Peru, and Guatemala, with plans to expand into seven more Latin American nations.

Among the many impressive female entrepreneurs Vital Voices supports are Guo Jianmei, who founded the first NGO in China devoted to protecting women's legal rights and highlighting abuses in the home or workplace or by government; Jaya Arunachalam, founder of the Working

Women's Forum in India, which over the last twenty-nine years has empowered 800,000 women through microcredit, political involvement, and access to education and health care for their children; Rita Chaikin, who discovered that Russian women she counseled at a rape crisis center in Kiryat Shmona had been trafficked from Russia into Israel, and who now works to stop the annual inflow of an estimated fifteen hundred to three thousand women into her country; and Inez McCormack, former Northern Ireland regional secretary of UNISON, the United Kingdom's largest trade union, which built the Equality Coalition to ensure that Northern Ireland's Good Friday Agreement would be fair to both Protestants and Catholics, to both women and men. With Vital Voices, Inez now brings Arab-Israeli and Jewish-Israeli women to Northern Ireland to better understand the opportunities of peace-building.

And there is Mukhtaran Bibi of Pakistan, who was gang-raped by order of an all-male tribunal in her village in retribution for her twelve-year-old brother allegedly holding hands with a girl from a higher-caste tribe. She was then forced to walk home naked in front of the villagers. Instead of committing suicide in shame, she pursued her attackers, was awarded compensation, and used the money to establish a primary school for girls and one for boys in her village. She too was illiterate, so she enrolled in her own elementary school to learn to read and write. She has also started her own aid organization and an ambulance service. Such women are worthy of our support.

Vital Voices is headquartered in Washington, D.C. Many of its financial supporters and volunteer activists are women. Think how much more they could accomplish with more money and more people.

In the United States, many citizens work individually or

in groups to help ease tensions, relieve suffering, provide educational and economic opportunities, and resolve conflicts in the nations where they have their ethnic, religious, and family roots. Indian Americans and Pakistanis; Greeks and Turks; Serbs, Croats, Bosnian Muslims, and Kosovars; Jews and Arabs; Irish Catholics and Irish Protestants—all have been active in efforts to give troubled places new beginnings. Almost all of them have achieved a fair measure of success in America, and some are quite wealthy, like my friends Haim Saban and Danny Abraham, who have established foundations to continue the search for a just and lasting peace in the Middle East. But you don't have to be wealthy—thousands of middle-class Americans also do what they can for their homelands. I'm not sure the conflict in Northern Ireland would have resolved itself by now had it not been for the years of devoted efforts by a very large number of Irish Americans to get America to play a more active role and to provide more economic opportunity for both Catholics and Protestants there. Despite the obstacles, I see that same commitment among other Americans to resolving the conflicts in the Middle East, in South Asia, and between Greece and Turkey over Cyprus.

Perhaps the most amazing reconciliation efforts in the world are those taking place in Rwanda. In 1994, killers from the Hutu majority slaughtered 800,000 Tutsis and their Hutu sympathizers in ninety days, mostly by using machetes. One of the greatest regrets of my presidency is that I did not send forces as a part of a U.N. mission to stop it. In 1998, when Hillary and I visited Rwanda, I apologized for not doing more sooner and asked to meet with survivors who were trying to put their country together again.

In a small room at the Kigali airport, six survivors told us their stories. The last speaker, Josephine Murebwayire, was a dignified woman who described how her family had been identified to the rampaging killers as Tutsis by Hutu neighbors whose children had for years played with hers. She was badly wounded by machete hacks across her back and left for dead. When she regained consciousness, she was lying in a pool of her own blood with her husband and six children dead beside her. She told Hillary and me she had cried out to God in despair that she had survived, then came to understand that "my life must have been spared for a reason, and it could not be something as mean as vengeance. So I do what I can to help us start again." She was raising six children who had lost their parents in the massacre.

Several times after leaving the White House, I went back to Rwanda, where my foundation has major AIDS and economic development projects. My friend Casey Wasserman and I also helped the Rwandans complete their memorial to the genocide. It has powerful exhibits in a simple but beautiful building that sits on a hillside in Kigali, the capital city. Into the hill are dug eleven large tombs containing the bones of more than 250,000 of the victims. I was given a tour of the exhibits by a handsome young man who told me he had lost more than seventy relatives in the killing, from his immediate family to aunts, uncles, and cousins. When I asked him if his loss made it difficult for him to work at the memorial, he said no, it was therapeutic because it helped him and those who visited to begin again. Then I told him about meeting the woman who had lost her husband and six children on my first trip in 1998 and said he reminded me of her. "I should," he said. "She's my aunt."

There are lots of stories like that in Rwanda. President Paul Kagame has established reconciliation villages in which Hutus and Tutsis live side by side. I visited one of them and saw a Hutu woman holding hands with her Tutsi neighbor whose husband and brother were killed. The Hutu woman's husband was in prison awaiting a war crimes trial for playing an important role in the genocide. I talked with a young Hutu who had come back from exile in the Congo when the president said low-level Hutu combatants could return if they confessed their crimes and did whatever community atonement service the village ordered them to do. The people I met had gathered at the home of a Hutu woman, who was caring for two orphaned Tutsi children who were bedridden, gravely ill with an incurable congenital medical condition.

Rwandan women have adopted between 400,000 and 500,000 orphans. Women comprise 49 percent of the lower house of Parliament, the highest percentage in the world. And they are making major contributions to the economic recovery of their country. Pascasie Mukamunigo is a Tutsi woman who lost her mother, brother, husband, and the youngest seven of her ten children. She also lost her life savings and her basket-weaving business. At fifty, she had to begin all over again. With a Hutu neighbor she recruited people into a basket-weaving collective that now has 120 members, including several men. One of her young basket makers eventually confessed to Pascasie that he had killed one of her sons. Racked with grief and guilt, he told her he would understand if one of her surviving sons killed him. Instead, she forgave him. When asked why, she said, "What good does revenge do me? What good does it do anyone? It doesn't help us to heal."

Pascasie's basket-weaving collective is called Agaseke K'amaho Ro, "Let's Hold on to Each Other." Her story is told in greater detail in Kimberley Sevcik and Beth O'Donnell's beautiful book, *Angels in Africa*.

One of the most endearing, poignant gifts of peace and

reconciliation I've ever encountered is the music of the Vallenato children of Colombia. Vallenato music springs from
the part of Colombia that borders the Caribbean, especially
the state of Cesar and its more than 450-year-old capital
city, Valledupar, which sits back from the coast in the mountainous tropical forest. For forty years, the area has been
plagued by some of the worst violence between guerrillas
and paramilitary forces, with many innocent victims, including children.

In spite of the constant threat of harm, children, ranging
in age from six to twelve, come from farms and poor rural
villages to learn Vallenato music at the school of Andres Gil,
who teaches them to play accordions, drums, and wash-
boards, the "orchestra" of their native culture. They play
and sing in small groups, wearing traditional clothing,
including (for the boys) two-tone straw hats. And they perform undaunted by the danger and determined that their
music, by keeping their culture alive, will help to overcome
death and destruction.

In my second term as president, I heard the Vallenato
children twice, once at a White House Christmas party, and
again when I visited Cartagena, Colombia, in 2000 to express
support for President Pastrana's efforts to end the long civil
conflict. The children played for us in an open plaza and
coaxed Pastrana, Chelsea, and me into dancing with them.

The Vallenato children's biggest promoter was the
Colombian culture minister, Consuelo Araujo. About a year
after I was in Cartagena, the FARC guerrillas, who hated the
defiance of the children but could do nothing to them, kidnapped Consuelo, took her deep into the mountains, and
murdered her on September 30, 2001. The children had
composed a song asking FARC to release her, but they
remained deaf to the music of peace.

In June 2002, I went back to Cartagena during the presidential transition from Andres Pastrana to Alvaro Uribe to urge the international businesses operating there not to give up on the country. When I got off the plane, the Vallenato children were there, still playing and singing and accompanied by the then minister of culture, Consuelo's thirty-one-year-old niece. Consuelo's widower had also joined government service, giving up his successful law practice to become a prosecutor, a very dangerous job in Colombia. My greeters gave me a brightly colored, hand-woven bracelet. Although almost no one does it, traditionally you're supposed to wear the bracelet until it wears out and falls off. More than five years later, I'm still wearing mine, a reminder of how brave the Colombians are, how determined they are to restore peace and preserve Latin America's oldest democracy, and how fortunate I am to live in a country without the daily threat of kidnapping and killing.

In the past five years I've seen the Vallenato children perform three more times, including at the dedication of my presidential library, where they shared a rain-drenched stage with Bono and The Edge of U2. They're wonderful, talented kids who've seen more than children their age should. Andres Gil has taught them well. But it is the power of their spirit that has touched the hearts of Colombians and made their two CDs best sellers. I wish every conflict area had a teacher like Maestro Gil and children like Los Niños Vallenatos.

Most people who will read this book live in places where the problems are less profound and visible than the agonizing ones I've written about. But there are people who need new beginnings everywhere. And there are good people and organizations trying to help them. If you live in a community with people from different ethnic and religious groups, your local school or congregation probably has a program to promote dialogue and understanding among the students. If there isn't such a program you could start one, perhaps working with an interested church, synagogue, mosque, or temple. Alcoholics Anonymous and other rehab programs, efforts to counsel and find jobs for former prison inmates, shelters that help battered women or families in distress—all are about new beginnings.

Historically, former prisoners have had a hard time starting again. They usually don't get much education or job training while incarcerated and even when they do, many employers are unwilling to hire them. Most don't have a home or a stable family to take them in. Without a job, they are likely to commit other crimes. The Ready4Work program is trying to change that. Ready4Work is a partnership between Public/Private Ventures, the Annie E. Casey and Ford foundations, the U.S. Department of Justice, and the U.S. Department of Labor. Since 2003, the project has worked with religious and nongovernmental groups and local government in seventeen cities to train newly released men and women, place them, and help them keep jobs. The results of their efforts have been impressive. Out of more than 4,800 returnees, only 1.9 percent of Ready4Work participants were incarcerated for a new offense within six months of their release, and only 5 percent were in jail within a year. In many states, the average recidivism rate in the first year is 20 percent. Moreover, the cost of the program is $4,500 per person a year, compared with $25,000 to $40,000 per year for incarceration.

Jacksonville, Florida, started its Ready4Work program when it received Department of Labor funding in 2003 under the leadership of Kevin Gay, who left a successful career as an insurance executive in 1999 to start his own NGO to redevelop a poor neighborhood in Jacksonville. All the newly released inmates get five weeks of basic training in job hunting, new suits for job interviews, and mentors, most of whom come from local churches. After the training period, the participants are matched with jobs, usually paying between $7 and $12 an hour, at one of one hundred participating employers.

One of Gay's success stories is Gerald Dove, Jr., a thirty-six-year-old former crack-cocaine dealer and multiple offender, who used his third stint in prison to learn various trades, help other inmates learn to read, and study to become a minister. He found a job making custom doors for Granger Lumber, paying $10 an hour. Dove's boss, Bob Bailey, had hired several inmates because he believes "if a young man made a mistake and paid for his mistake, he deserves a second chance."

It's difficult to overrate the importance of giving people like Gerald Dove that second chance. As Dove himself said, "It's hard for a person to be something they've never seen. I had never seen a successful man or woman who shared a similar history to mine until I came here." Ready4Work is succeeding in Florida. Just one in twenty of its participants is arrested within a year of release, compared with one in five of all those who are released from Florida's prisons.

Getting an education while in prison further reduces the chances that an inmate will commit another crime when released. Before 1995, there were about 350 college-degree programs for prisoners. Today there are fewer than twenty, because Congress, over my administration's opposition, eliminated Pell grants for state and federal prisoners in 1994. Four of the remaining programs are in New York, thanks to the Bard Prison Initiative, a privately funded effort organized by 2001 Bard graduate Max Kenner. The four programs have about 120 students, only 10 percent of those who apply for them.

Prison officials say inmates involved in education are much better behaved. Their professors say they work hard to learn the material. The student inmates say they love the classes. Why? In April 2007, Reshawn Hughes told *60 Minutes*, "While at Bard, I learned that freedom is something much different than just a physicality, a space of physical existence. Freedom had a lot [to] do with your ability to think. Freedom has a lot to do with your ability to communicate with others. To see the world in a different view." Mika'il DeVeaux, who founded Citizens Against Recidivism with his wife after studying theology while a prisoner at Sing Sing and getting an MA in sociology, says a college education is the surest way to close the revolving door of crime and imprisonment. The Bard Initiative costs $2,000 per inmate per year, compared with New York's incarceration cost of $32,000. It's a good investment in a safer, more productive society.

We have more than two million people incarcerated, more than any other Western country. The vast majority are imprisoned for nonviolent offenses. More than 90 percent of them will eventually get out. Each year 750,000 prisoners, including 150,000 juveniles, are released. Theoretically, they have paid their debt to society and are entitled to a new beginning. Too few of our fellow citizens are willing to give it to them. Thankfully, Ready4Work, the Bard Prison Initiative, and Citizens Against Recidivism do.

Wintley Phipps, one of America's best-known gospel singers, founded the U.S. Dream Academy to help the children of inmates avoid becoming collateral damage. Sixty to seventy percent of the children of prisoners eventually wind up in prison too. Phipps created his U.S. Dream Academy to break the cycle he had seen play out all too painfully in his own family's life: all seven of his wife's brothers and sisters had spent time in jail. The academy focuses on children in grades two through eight, offering mentoring, tutoring, and access to computers and the Internet. The mentors offer the children positive role models and work to build their self-esteem with affection and positive reinforcement. Wintley wants these children "to find their own voice and their own path in life." There are now ten Dream Academy Learning Centers across America, including two in Washington, D.C., where the program started. If your community has a U.S. Dream Academy, you might want to volunteer to be a mentor. You'll be giving a chance to kids before they get in trouble.

Many churches are directly involved in this kind of giving. The Pentecostals of Alexandria, a large Pentecostal church in central Louisiana, is a particularly impressive example. Its Grace House affords homeless men, including those recently incarcerated, the chance to build a new life for themselves. At any given time, Grace House can provide food, shelter, alcohol and drug abuse education, and life-skills training to sixteen men. The residents go through a three-phase program on the way to independence. During the first thirty days, residents are not allowed to leave the premises, except to attend church or approved meetings and classes. They cook, clean, mow the lawn, and perform other tasks. In the second phase, the men are allowed to seek and secure jobs, open a bank account, and get a driver's license. They can also, if they choose, become involved in church activities. To enter the final phase, the resident must receive the approval of two-thirds of those living with him at the shelter. At this point, they can drive, develop outside relationships, and help run Grace House.

Over the last two decades, nearly five thousand men have been through Grace House. In addition to leading productive lives, many have remained active members of the church. Harris Washington had been arrested numerous times—for everything from drugs to assault to robbery to resisting arrest. He was sleeping under a bridge when he found Grace House, more than ten years ago. Today, he has a home, a job, and a ministry. And he contributes $500 a year to Grace House. In 1997, John Russell had gone from being a star basketball player to an alcohol and drug addict, reduced to scavenging for food in dumpsters. After standing on a bridge over the Red River contemplating suicide, he sought shelter in the halls of a nearby hospital, where he overheard someone talking on the phone about Grace House. He found his way there. Today, John Russell is married with two children and works full-time for the Pentecostals of Alexandria. He oversees the church's House of Mercy, Grace House's counterpart for homeless women; gives motivational speeches to young people; and leads weekly religious services in a nearby prison. One of his success stories at House of Mercy was a drug addict who had lost custody of her children. She now has a job, a car, and an apartment. And, most important, she has her children back.

When Hurricanes Katrina and Rita hit the Gulf Coast, the church collected money, food, and other supplies for victims, and worked with the Red Cross to house more than three hundred of the evacuees at its campground for several weeks. Among them was an African-American family, Charles and Ovelia Haywood and their two teenage children. They decided to remain in Alexandria, and Charles is now a full-time member of the church staff, further integrating both its congregation and staff, still a rare phenomenon in the South.

Besides Grace House, House of Mercy, and its hurricane relief efforts, the Pentecostals of Alexandria runs a number of other outreach programs for needy people. Here is what the minister, Rev. Anthony Mangun, told me about their commitment to new beginnings: "This church works daily as if there is a disaster. If I pray for anything for your book, it is that it will convey the importance of coming together—the values of giving over receiving—and the power that lies in each of us to reach out to someone and change a life, and thereby change the world."

This is one story of people who believe that God has called on them to give new beginnings. It represents a kind of giving done every day in every community in the United States and countless places across the world. These givers are easy to find, and they always need volunteers.

I CLOSE THIS chapter with perhaps the most meaningful new-beginnings project I've ever participated in, the fundraising efforts with former President George H. W. Bush for the victims of Hurricane Katrina and the tsunami in southern Asia.

For the tsunami, we tried to raise the overall level of giving in America and put together a relatively small fund of about $14 million, out of which we financed the reconstruction of schools, health facilities, fishing boats, and other economic restoration efforts, and scholarships for students from Aceh in Indonesia, by far the hardest-hit area, to study at Texas A&M and the University of Arkansas.

The Bush-Clinton Katrina Fund raised more than $130 million, of which $40 million was allocated to states to fill in gaps in federal programs; $30 million to institutions of higher education, many of which were damaged by the hurricane; $25 million to interfaith groups; and just over $35 million to direct grants for a variety of programs, including support for distressed local governments, helping

Alabama shrimpers whose boats were blown onto land repair them and get them back into the water, providing mental health services, and, for New Orleans, rebuilding schools as green buildings, funding charter schools and more Teach for America members, and establishing a City Year youth service chapter.

The efforts George Bush and I made to help people begin again benefited more than those who received the funds. It also gave us the opportunity to rebuild a friendship that began almost twenty-five years ago, when he was vice president and I was a young governor. We've had a lot of fun traveling around the United States and the world. Although we still have our political differences, we can laugh about them now, even when arguing. I never forget that George Bush is eighty-three (though he's still parachuting out of airplanes!) and has now given more than sixty years of service to his country, beginning as a pilot in World War II. I should be doing this kind of work, but he could easily take a pass. Instead he keeps volunteering.

Our partnership seemed to strike a responsive chord in America and around the world, I think because it was an affirmation of our common humanity—not just his and mine as former opponents, but the essential humanity that we all share but too easily forget until something bad happens.

I'm still involved in a more limited way with the rebuilding efforts in New Orleans, and George and I got so excited by our tsunami work that we both wound up working on disasters two more years for U.N. secretary general Kofi Annan. I became the U.N. envoy for the tsunami restoration efforts; George did the same thing in Pakistan after the earthquake there.

On one of my trips to Indonesia, I had an experience that brought home more clearly than ever the meaning of new beginnings. I went to a settlement where people were still uncomfortably living in tents. On my tour, I was accompanied by my interpreter, a lively young woman who had been a reporter on Indonesian television, and the elected leader of the residents, who met me at the camp entrance with his wife and young son.

The boy was a stunningly beautiful child, with enormous brown eyes and a blinding smile. I told the interpreter I thought he might be the most beautiful child I'd ever seen. "Yes, he is very beautiful," she replied, "and before the tsunami he had nine brothers and sisters, and they're all gone." Yet the father had a smile on his face and talked not about his grief but about the needs of the people he represented.

The last stop on the tour was the health clinic. When I was there, the leader's wife came up to me, holding a little boy less than a week old. The baby's mother, in keeping with their custom, was resting in bed, something she would do for forty days. The woman who had lost nine of her own children was smiling when she said, "This is our newest baby. We want you to name him." I asked her if there was an Indonesian word for "new beginning." The woman beamed again and through the interpreter said, "Yes. In our language, the word 'dawn' is a boy's name, not a girl's. We will call this child Dawn, and he will symbolize our new beginning."

The world is awash in divisions rooted in the human compulsion to believe our differences are more important than our common humanity. The next time you're tempted to give in to it, or wonder why you should give your time, money, and effort to new beginnings, think of those brave parents who lost nine children, cherished the one left behind, and in the midst of all their adversity, named a newborn baby Dawn.

SEVEN

Gifts That Keep on Giving

———

NEXT DOOR TO my library in Little Rock, Arkansas, is the world headquarters of Heifer International, founded in 1944 by Dan West, who was a relief worker during the Spanish Civil War. That experience convinced him that what poor and suffering people really need far more than temporary help is the ability to support themselves. So he began shipping them cows.

Sixty-three years later, Heifer has evolved into one of the world's most successful and widely acclaimed givers for two reasons. First, it works to end world hunger by giving cows, goats, and other food and income-producing livestock and agricultural goods to poor families around the world. The animals are now bought locally to maximize resistance to local diseases and to help local economies. They produce milk, eggs, wool, and meat, enhancing nutrition and earning money for education, health care, better housing, and small-business endeavors. Heifer partners with local groups to ensure that the agriculture it supports is sustainable, promoting animal health, and water quality, soil conservation, and efficient energy use. Heifer also champions equality for women and community development.

Fittingly, because of its commitment to a sustainable environment, the new international headquarters was built making maximum use of recycled materials, capturing and using rainwater, and conserving energy. I believe that the Heifer headquarters and my library, which has a LEED (Leadership in Energy and Environmental Design) silver certification from the U.S. Green Building Council, will soon be the only two adjacent headquarters buildings in America to receive one of the top two LEED certifications.

The second reason for Heifer's success is that those who receive its animals are required to share the first offspring with others in need, thus multiplying the impact of all donated animals and making their recipients partners in the struggle against hunger and poverty. Since 1944, Heifer has given animals to 10 million people, but through the ritual of "Passing on the Gift," it has helped more than 45 million people in 128 countries around the world, with plans to reach 23 million more by the end of the decade. Heifer's message and methods go out to millions of others every year through the media, its own publications, and its three learning centers in the United States, where fifty thousand people annually are taught how to serve small farmers through teaching sustainable practices like organic gardening and alternative marketing methods.

In 2006, Heifer had 726 projects in twenty-nine states in the United States and fifty-seven countries in Latin America and the Caribbean, Africa, central and eastern Europe, the Asia-Pacific region, Canada, and Mexico. In addition to its gifts of cows, goats, sheep, turkeys, pigs, and fish, the animals it supplies include agouti, alpacas, bees, camels, ducks, earthworms, elephants, geese, guinea fowl, guinea pigs, horses, llamas, mules, oxen, rabbits, silkworms, snails, water buffalo, and yaks.

Heifer's animals dramatically improve the lives of poor people. Elmfus Lembusha, a Tanzanian farmer, was trying to support an extended family of sixteen on an acre of farmland when Heifer sent him goats to produce milk and manure to make the land more productive, improve the family's nutrition, and provide them with a steady cash income. A river village in the Dominican Republic forced to relocate by a dam construction project survived and prospered when Heifer gave the villagers goats and trained them in how to care for the animals and how to make the soil fertile for growing livestock feed. A Kenyan widow with three children received a cow that restored her family's health and income. In northern Peru, Heifer provided families not only with animals but also with fuel-efficient kitchen stoves that are safer than open fires and don't require cutting trees for firewood.

When I spoke at the dedication of the Heifer World Headquarters in 2006, one of the beneficiaries in the audience was Beatrice Biira of Kisinga, a small village on the equator in western Uganda. In the early 1990s, Beatrice, her parents, and five brothers and sisters were struggling to survive when they received one of twelve goats Heifer donated to Kisinga. Beatrice had always wanted to go to school, but her family was too poor to afford the school fees. Within a year her mother had earned enough money selling goat's milk to pay the fees. Eventually, she was able to send all the rest of her children to school with her earnings from selling milk and the goat's offspring (after passing on the gift of the first one).

Beatrice completed the first three grades in three months each, showing such promise that Dick Young, producer of a Heifer documentary film that featured her village, helped pay for her enrollment at a more advanced school in Kampala, Uganda's capital. From there she went for a year to a prestigious American prep school, Northfield Mount Hermon in Massachusetts, then on to Connecticut College on a scholarship. While there, Beatrice served as an intern in Hillary's Senate office. She has been featured on *60 Minutes* and by Oprah Winfrey, a Heifer supporter. Her remarkable story is chronicled in *Beatrice's Goat*, an engaging children's book written by Page McBrier and illustrated by Lori Lohstoeter. Beatrice wants to go home and use her education to benefit her people by forming a school for poor kids, taking care of AIDS orphans, or running a farm that helps other children the way Heifer helped her and her family.

It all started with a goat named Mugisa (which means "Luck"). But it didn't end there, because Beatrice's family and the other eleven families completed their obligation to pass on the gift, putting twelve more families on the path to working themselves out of poverty.

Passing on the gift turns every Heifer recipient into a better citizen and a mini-NGO. A Nepalese women's group, Gurung Gaon, used a Heifer water buffalo to improve their lot. Beyond passing on the offspring, the women saved enough of their income to buy one hundred geese for five families in China. The group leader, Leela Tamang, said, "Before Heifer, I didn't know what sharing was." Ghanaian farmer Anthony Gygrengye Kodom and his wife, Mercy Dansua, are members of a farmers' group supported by Heifer. In 2005, they received twenty chickens and five beehives and passed on their gift within just seven months, then grew their operation to include more than seven hundred laying hens and twenty-five beehives. They also went beyond their gift requirement, providing land to their farmers' cooperative for communal chicken coops. Women in a Heifer project in Zimbabwe passed on twice as many pigs as required because they wanted more women to enjoy the same prosperity they did. In the Dominican Republic fifty-eight families have gone so far beyond the requirement that those receiving dairy cattle have increased more than ten-fold, to 650 families.

When I was back in Arkansas for the Heifer headquarters opening, one of the local TV stations ran a story on black farmers in the Mississippi Delta passing on the first offspring of Heifer-provided cows. As governor and as president, I tried to help farmers like them who wanted to hold on to their farms or get back into farming. More of them will do so because of Heifer's gifts and the practice of passing them on.

Just a decade ago, Heifer was still a modest operation, raising $6 to $7 million a year. In 2006, contributions reached $80 million, thanks to good publicity, celebrity support, effective marketing, and energetic and visionary leadership. The Heifer president, Jo Luck, is passionate and relentless in her pursuit of supporters and new recipients. She's equally comfortable talking to corporate CEOs and celebrities and sitting on the ground in Africa, Asia, and Latin America listening to villagers talk about their lives.

Heifer's rapid growth doesn't mean the organization can't use your support. Remember, nearly a billion people still live on less than a dollar a day, and about 820 million go to bed hungry every night. There is virtually no limit to the good Heifer can do. Donors know the program works. And best of all, by turning every beneficiary into a donor, your gift just keeps on giving.

Nearly everyone can make a meaningful contribution. You can give a heifer for $500 or a share of one for $50; a water buffalo for $250, or a share for $25; a llama for $150, or a share for $20; a sheep, goat, or pig for $120, or a share for $10; a trio of rabbits for $60; bees, a beehive, and a training kit for $30; a group of ducks, geese, or chickens for $20.

Young students who want to contribute to Heifer can participate in Read to Feed, in which sponsors pay them for the books they read. Last year the effort raised $1.2 million.

I have devoted an entire chapter to Heifer because I believe that if the concept of "Passing on the Gift" were to be integrated into other giving programs wherever possible, it would dramatically increase the impact of good works at almost no cost. What if all the givers of money, time, and skills required the recipients of their gifts to do something, however modest, for others in similar situations? In a sense, that's what happens when those who benefit from NGO leadership-training programs will pass along the skills they've learned. Of course, it won't work in all cases. Infants with AIDS, for instance, are giving back enough if they just survive and go on to a normal childhood. But there are many other efforts in which the positive value of giving could be multiplied by asking the beneficiaries to pass on the gift.

For example, at the midyear meeting of the Clinton Global Initiative in April 2007, the crowd was brought to its feet by a beautifully eloquent seventeen-year-old South African girl who had been helped by the Ubuntu Education Fund, which provides support to orphans and vulnerable children (*ubuntu* means "I am because you are" in the Xhosa language). Zethu lost both her parents to AIDS a few years ago and assumed the responsibility for raising her two young siblings with no idea even of how to feed them. An Ubuntu caseworker, Fezeka Mzalazala, helped Zethu to stay in school and work through her emotional and financial problems. After experiencing how Fezeka's support enabled her to turn her life around, Zethu said she wanted to "spread the spirit of Ubuntu" by creating a support group for ten younger orphaned girls to discuss the issues they face, help them cope, and bring them the benefits of Ubuntu counseling. Zethu found a way to pass on her gift.

In the United States, the best example I've found of passing on the gift is the Page Education Foundation. Founded in 1988 by Alan and Diane Page, it offers scholarships to deserving students of color in Minnesota to help them with the costs of a post-secondary education. During his fifteen-year career in the NFL, which earned him a place in the Pro Football Hall of Fame, Alan earned a law degree. After leaving professional football, he was elected a justice of the Minnesota Supreme Court. He and Diane wanted to give other young people of color the chance to develop their potential: "We know there is no shortage of potential—only a shortage of appropriate support and encouragement." Since its inception, the Page Foundation has provided more than $6 million in grants to 3,000 Page scholars, almost 600 in 2006 alone.

In return for the grant, every Page scholar agrees to spend at least fifty hours an academic year mentoring or tutoring younger children of color from kindergarten through eighth grade. Many volunteer well above the fifty-hour requirement in established programs operated by schools, libraries, and community organizations. In 2006, the scholars helped more than ten thousand children. In so doing, they provided young children with both academic support and vivid role models of what they can become if they stay in school and apply themselves. It's a wonderful way of passing on the gift.

Bernard Rapoport, the legendary ninety-year-old Texas philanthropist and social activist, and his wife, Audre, agree. They give about $400,000 a year in "service learning" scholarships—with a community-service component—to University of Texas students. Students are required to immediately pass on their gift, and in so doing, to enhance their own learning.

If you're already involved in service work, I hope you'll think about whether and how those you're trying to help can also pass on their gifts.

EIGHT

Model Gifts

———

ONE THING THAT makes programs as diverse as Heifer International, the Self Employed Women's Association in India, and New York's Chess-in-the-Schools so appealing to givers is that they're repeatable models that virtually always work. You know that if there are more animals, more microloans, more chess programs, those who receive them will be better off in predictable but gratifying ways. You don't have to invent or reinvent the wheel; you just provide the money or volunteer time to bring the benefits of such programs to more people. Whenever I read about, observe, or participate in an exciting new project, I ask myself whether it can be replicated with predictable positive results and, if so, how.

In cases where different kinds of resources are required to achieve multiple goals, constructing such models is more difficult. That's what Dr. Paul Farmer's Partners In Health and my foundation's HIV/AIDS Initiative are trying to do in Rwanda. Yes, we want to bring quality health care to people in isolated villages. But we also want to be able to say, "It works in Haiti. It works in Rwanda. This is the best, fastest, most cost-effective way to get health care to poor people everywhere. Please give money and time to spread it to everyone who needs it."

In this chapter, I discuss some important efforts that could become repeatable models. Those that pursue several objectives at the same time present significant challenges to donors in terms of time, skills, or money, but they're all worthy of support just for what they're doing, and they have at least the potential to be greatly expanded.

In 2000, the United Nations adopted the Millennium Development Goals. It pledged to cut in half the number of people living in extreme poverty (less than $1 a day) by 2015; to reduce by half the number of people suffering from hunger; to ensure all children at least a primary school education (each year of schooling adds 10 percent a year to the income of a person in a poor country); to end the disparity in school attendance between boys and girls; to reduce mortality among children under five by two-thirds and maternal mortality by three-quarters; to cut in half the number of people without access to clean water; and to halt and begin to reverse the incidence of HIV/AIDS, TB, malaria, and other major infectious diseases.

In 1999, the G8, the world's major economic powers, launched the millennium debt relief initiative to forgive the debts of the poorest highly indebted nations if they protected human rights and agreed to put all their savings into education, health, or economic development. In 2005, the G8 leaders pledged another round of debt relief and promised to double aid to Africa, to $50 billion per year. But no one believes that even these big steps will be enough to enable the poorest African nations to reach the Millennium Development Goals. Almost half the people in sub-

Saharan Africa are living in poverty, about one-third are malnourished, more than 300 million people live on less than $1 a day, and the support systems necessary for success are often inadequate or nonexistent. Where to start? Dr. Jeffrey Sachs, a renowned Columbia University economist who was U.N. secretary general Kofi Annan's special advisor on the Millennium Development Goals, has for years been promoting the concept of Millennium Villages as the best way for public and private aid to help poor people work themselves out of poverty. And he believes each village can do it in five years.

The villages work to increase food production; improve nutrition, especially for pregnant women, nursing mothers, and infants; provide basic health care, education, and clean water; promote gender equality; and eliminate the digital divide. The first village, launched in 2004 in Sauri, Kenya, saw a tripling of crop production, with villagers moving from chronic hunger to selling their products in nearby markets. A second village in Ethiopia achieved similar results. The government of Japan provided funding for an additional ten villages in other African nations. As of mid-2007, there were seventy-nine of them.

Private donors can now contribute to increasing the number of villages through Millennium Promise, an NGO working with the U.N. Development Program and other partners. George Soros has pledged millions to the effort, but you don't have to be as wealthy as he is to make a measurable difference. Each Millennium Village requires a total private donor investment of $250,000 for a village of five thousand people. That means someone who gives $50 to Millennium Promise can help sponsor one villager in a Millennium Village for a year.

The villages have already produced some impressive results. In Sauri, a young man who returned home after losing his job at a textile factory received good seed, fertilizer, and instructions on how to manage his crops. He greatly increased his yield, diversified his crops, added livestock, and installed bed nets in his home to protect his five children against malaria. In Ghana, Millennium Promise gives seeds and fertilizer to farmers and requires them, in return, to donate 10 percent of their produce to the nation's school-feeding program, which often provides a child's only meal (a good example of "Passing on the Gift"). In Ikaram, Nigeria, after five fallow years, farmers are growing bananas, pumpkins, yams, tomatoes, and chili as well as the standard maize, cassava, and beans. Undernourishment has decreased significantly. Millennium Promise is chipping away at the Millennium Development Goals one village at a time.

There are similar efforts elsewhere designed to develop a national model to eliminate extreme poverty and substantially increase per capita income. One of these was inspired and is funded by the Scottish philanthropist Sir Tom Hunter. Hunter started his business career as a young man, selling running shoes out of his small van. By 1998, his operation had grown into Sports Division, a network of more than 250 sports apparel stores. He sold it for £290 million and with his wife, Marion, established the Hunter Foundation, which initially supported education and economic empowerment in Scotland. By the time I met him a couple of years ago, he had developed and funded, in partnership with the Scottish government, an economic education program for all Scottish primary school children. Tom was also active in mobilizing popular support for Prime Minister Tony Blair's proposal to have the G8 promote doubling aid to Africa and debt relief for poor nations at its annual conference hosted by the United Kingdom at Gleneagles, Scotland, in 2005.

Hunter is a fascinating character. Compact, intelligent,

intense, blunt, and just forty-six years old, he looks as if he'd be more at home on a rugby pitch than in a boardroom. He joined me on a trip to Africa in 2005, and I was struck by the similarities in our approach: we both believe in programs that have a large impact within a reasonably short time frame at the least possible cost. He told me he wanted to give away a great deal of money without wasting any: "I am Scottish, you know." We talked on that trip about the good results his enterprise education efforts had achieved in poor neighborhoods in Scotland, and agreed that poor people everywhere could do well if they had the skills and basic systems necessary to succeed. Over the next few months our discussions grew into the Clinton-Hunter Development Initiative to spark substantial and sustainable economic growth in Africa.

At the inaugural meeting of the Clinton Global Initiative, Hunter committed up to $100 million over ten years, and we decided to work on developing national growth strategies beginning in Rwanda and Malawi. In both cases the governments asked us to come in, pledged full cooperation, and assured us that our work was consistent with their own development strategies.

Our mission is to develop programs that produce profits from agriculture; ensure more access to nutrition, clean water, and health care; can be expanded nationwide; and eventually can be fully supported by local communities and the national government without outside help. Our work began in eastern Rwanda, in a poor dry region of 425,000 people, and in three regions in Malawi with a total population of 584,000. In all these areas, most people rely on agriculture for survival.

In Rwanda, CHDI improved agricultural productivity by increasing the use of fertilizer, disease-resistant seeds, advanced planting techniques, irrigation, and microcredit;

by cultivating markets for the produce and developing value-added farm products; by providing more access to clean water, especially in health clinics and schools; and by strengthening the health-care systems working with Partners In Health.

Even though the program has been under way only a year, farmers in Rwanda enjoyed a 240 percent increase in maize harvests and created a significant surplus thanks to fertilizer, new seeds, advanced planting, and good rains. CHDI worked with the Rwandan government to import a record fourteen thousand tons of fertilizer at a 30 percent discount, and negotiated lower interest rates of microcredit loans for farmers and cooperatives, enabling many farmers to purchase their own fertilizer and seeds for the first time. These steps are helping to establish food security for thousands of families. In Malawi, at the government's request, we began by improving the health infrastructure, training community health workers, and supporting treatment for 3,500 HIV-positive children.

CHDI will continue to expand in Rwanda, working with farmers to extend cash crops including soybeans; strengthen agricultural cooperatives; prepare irrigation and development plans for hillside terrain; provide clean water and sanitation to ten schools and five health facilities; and encouraging the banking sector to support farm cooperatives' access to credit and launch a program for carbon offsets benefiting agriculture and planting trees in areas that have been deforested. In Malawi, CHDI plans to provide clean water and sanitation to seventeen more hospitals and twenty schools; expand clean water and sanitation in poor villages; develop plans for new crops and a strategy for marketing them; provide more adequate nutrition to children; and build the capacity of the national health system to test for and treat malaria. In both nations we are exploring ways to improve land management and expand the use of renewable energy. In 2008, we hope to expand these efforts to other regions in Rwanda and Malawi, and begin work in a third country. We have actively solicited other partners, including ShoreBank of Chicago. Will it work? Can we develop and implement a comprehensive strategy that will lift the per capita income of an entire country and eliminate extreme poverty? I don't know, but it's worth a try. So far, a great many people are better off, and Tom Hunter is getting his money's worth.

Another economic initiative just launched in Liberia has the potential to become a model that can be implemented in other countries. The Liberia Enterprise Development Fund (LEDF) was organized by Bob Johnson, founder of Black Entertainment Television and majority owner of the Charlotte Bobcats professional basketball team. After fourteen years of a bloody civil war that left the small West African nation of three million in ruins, Liberians elected Ellen Johnson-Sirleaf president. A Harvard graduate, former World Bank official, onetime political prisoner and then political exile in Liberia's dark years, Johnson-Sirleaf, a grandmother of six, is called the "Iron Lady" by her supporters. In 2005, after serving as head of Liberia's Governance Reform Commission, she won a hotly contested election against a former soccer star backed by supporters of the previous regime.

After she spoke at the Clinton Global Initiative in 2006 about Liberia's troubles and dreams, Bob Johnson decided he wanted to help. He thought that since Liberia had been founded by freed American slaves, African-American businesspeople should help to spur its revival. Johnson committed to capitalize the Liberia Enterprise Development Fund at $30 million; to work with the U.S. Overseas Private Investment Corporation and the U.S.-African Development Foundation to maximize its impact; and to designate CHF International to manage the fund's operation in Liberia. CHF has been promoting economic development in the United States and more than one hundred other countries since the early 1950s, with an excellent track record in community building.

The fund will focus on promoting enterprise and creating jobs through loans, equity investments, and technical assistance to local business and new entrepreneurs, and will mobilize funds for health, education, and agricultural programs. Johnson has already enlisted other prominent African-American business executives to participate, including music executive Clarence Avant, president and COO of BET Debra Lee, former transportation secretary Rodney Slater, and actors Chris Tucker, Cicely Tyson, and Jeffrey Wright.

When I went to Liberia during the summer of 2006 to kick off my foundation's HIV/AIDS program there, President Johnson-Sirleaf asked me to meet with some university students. I spoke for a few minutes and answered their questions for about an hour. The young people I met were as intelligent, informed, articulate, and future-oriented as any college group I have ever encountered. They were looking past the years of killing, even past the economic ruin left in its wake. Anyone who met them would want to support Liberia's rebirth.

If you want to participate, you will find the fund's Web site at the end of the book. You'll be doing good, and you might be building a model that will catch on.

One of the biggest challenges confronting any assistance effort in another country is adapting good intentions to the habits, values, and aspirations of the local culture. No one has done it better and under more adverse circumstances than Greg Mortenson and his Central Asia Institute.

In 1993, Mortenson was descending from a failed attempt to reach the peak of the world's second-highest mountain, K2 in Pakistan's rugged Karakoram Mountains. He was exhausted and disoriented. He wandered away from his group and wound up in a poor Pakistani village, where he recovered his health. While there, he saw the village children outdoors, trying to learn without a paid teacher, books, or learning materials. He promised to return and build them a school.

When he got back to the United States, he sold virtually all he owned for just $2,000. He wrote letters to nearly six hundred celebrities for help. Only Tom Brokaw sent him a check for $100. Then elementary school students in River Falls, Wisconsin, gave him $623 in pennies. After that, adults started to help. In 1996, Dr. Jean Hoerni, a Silicon Valley microchip entrepreneur, gave Mortenson a large amount of money to establish the Central Asia Institute, and the work took off. By 2007, Mortenson and the Institute had established fifty-eight schools in Pakistan and Afghanistan and had educated more than 24,000 children, including 14,000 girls. They have also trained teachers and established libraries.

Mortenson's work is a potential model for others for two reasons. First, its projects are entirely initiated, implemented, and managed by local communities, empowering local people and dramatically increasing the chance of success.

Second, the program is financed by very small as well as large contributors, providing children in the United States the chance to contribute and learn how different life is for kids in poor nations. Pennies for Peace solicits pennies from schoolchildren over a fixed period of time, usually two or three months. Only pennies are collected and students learn that, while a penny won't buy anything in the United States anymore, it buys a pencil and opens doors to literacy in Pakistan and Afghanistan. Many other NGOs could involve kids in this way, harnessing their energy to help others, teaching them about the needs in their community and the world, and cultivating the next generation of givers.

Mortenson has chronicled his "mission to promote peace, one school at a time" in his fine book, *Three Cups of Tea*.

IN THE UNITED STATES, the Local Initiatives Support Corporation (LISC) has been working with distressed communities since 1980 to promote the same kind of comprehensive economic progress the Millennium Development Goals envision for poor nations. LISC works through local community development corporations to create affordable housing, commercial, industrial, and community facilities, businesses, and jobs. It provides loans, grants, and equity investments, technical and management assistance, and support for more helpful government policies.

I am always surprised by how few Americans have heard about LISC's remarkable work. Since 1980, LISC has raised more than $7.8 billion from 3,100 investors, lenders, and donors. The funds have been put to use in more than 300 urban neighborhoods and rural communities to help 2,800 organizations build or rehabilitate more than 196,000 affordable houses and nearly 30 million square feet of retail, community, and educational space. LISC operations have created more than 70,000 jobs, helped more than 100 businesses, developed 53 supermarkets and farmers' markets, built 120 child-care facilities for 11,000 kids, renovated 136 playing fields serving 120,000 children, and financed 80 schools for 28,000 students.

Since 2003, LISC has worked to make the most of the 25 percent New Markets Tax Credit for investments in commercial projects, museums, and artist spaces in poor neighborhoods and rural communities. It's a great incentive, but most investors don't know about it. So far LISC has invested in nine New Markets projects in several states. LISC also has a Green Development Center to support green design, construction, and management in low- and moderate-income neighborhoods. This is particularly important, because greener buildings lower utility bills, raise home values, save money for schools to invest in learning, and expose people to fewer toxic substances.

I am especially proud of two other LISC efforts using AmeriCorps volunteers and helping communities damaged by Hurricanes Katrina, Rita, and Wilma. Since 1994, LISC has enlisted one thousand AmeriCorps volunteers in eighteen cities from Boston to Los Angeles. In the hurricane-affected areas, it has already provided more than $100 million in loans, grants, and equity, repaired 610 homes, assisted 1,000 evacuee families, raised $7.5 million for community development, and started building more than 2,400 homes.

When he resigned as treasury secretary to return to private life, Bob Rubin became chairman of the board of LISC. In the White House and at Treasury, Bob supported my initiatives to encourage more investment in low- and moderate-income communities. These efforts helped almost eight million Americans to move from poverty to the middle class—after twelve years in which poverty rates had increased. He's still doing that with his partners at LISC.

If you're an investor who wants a proven model for doing

well by doing good, you should contact LISC for opportunities. If you don't have that kind of money but want more productive investment in your community, rural or urban, you can get involved with your local Community Development Corporation. Community Development Corporations have been around since the first one was established in 1967 in Brooklyn's Bedford-Stuyvesant section with the support of Senator Robert Kennedy. As more and more community activists saw how the development corporations could be used to develop safe, decent housing and new jobs, they spread across America. There are more than four thousand Community Development Corporations today, with a wealth of experiences to be shared. They are really just investment vehicles that can be used to meet whatever the most pressing needs are. If your city or town doesn't have one, you can set one up as a charitable 501(c)3 corporation, decide what you want to accomplish, and contact LISC about opportunities to work together.

The Urban Enterprise Initiative is a much smaller example of community development that focuses on helping new and established small businesses in Harlem. The UEI grew out of conversations I had with leaders of the small-business community after I opened my foundation office there. They told me that even long-established businesses were having a hard time because of rising rents, competition from large chain stores, and rapid changes in consumer markets.

My office contacted Reggie Van Lee, a senior partner at Booz Allen Hamilton, who took the lead in putting together a set of pro bono teams of Booz Allen consultants, graduate students from New York University's Stern School of Business, and partner organizations including the National Black MBA Association.

Since 2002, UEI teams have supported thirty-five businesses in Harlem, Brooklyn, and the Bronx, donating more than fifty thousand hours of services worth more than $12 million. The teams work with their clients for a year, first conducting a thorough assessment of their financial condition and business practices, then developing specific strategies to address the problems and expand the opportunities, and finally testing the plan with the business owner, adjusting it as appropriate, and developing systems to measure performance and sustain progress after the consulting period is over.

Sometimes the plans have involved simple changes like converting month-to-month leases to year-long ones, improving inventory management, or just computerizing operations. One team helped an African-American-woman-owned architecture firm develop a long-term growth strategy to boost day-to-day efficiency. Another helped a café open a new location, brand itself more clearly, and resolve conflicts with its contractor. A custom cabinetmaker got assistance to improve its manufacturing process to cut costs and increase output, while arranging for its Spanish-speaking staff to learn English, further boosting worker productivity. A plumbing business was reorganized so that more calls could be answered, increasing revenues and profits. In 2006, my foundation and UEI launched a partnership with *Inc.* magazine to provide peer mentors to nine emerging entrepreneurs, some of whom are alumni of the consulting program. The businesses include a microbrewery, a boutique hat shop, an ad agency, and Harlem's first bowling alley in decades.

All this may sound simple, but most small-business owners work long hours for modest incomes. They don't have the time or money to examine their operations or get the kind of regular advice the consultants and *Inc.* mentors offer. Big companies pay major consulting firms large fees to review their operations and boost their CEO's effectiveness in this way.

This is hard work with no guarantees of success. A client survey of twelve businesses showed that UEI had an enormously positive impact on three, a moderately positive impact on four, and no impact on five, either because our team couldn't help or the business owner decided not to follow through on the program. Is it worth the effort? It's a great learning experience for the business school students, and other UEI volunteers who have worked on successful projects feel they've done something important. The *Inc.* mentors seem to be having a great time. They're an impressive group, including Jay Goltz, who built the largest picture framing business in the United States, and Pete Slosberg, who built Pete's Brewing Company into one of *Inc.* magazine's "Top 100 Companies" for three straight years.

I'd like to expand the UEI throughout New York and see similar programs set up in other cities, but doing so would require some investment capital. It's unrealistic to expect many companies to give the huge amounts of time and resources Booz Allen has devoted to UEI. But with enough money to fund a small staff to recruit and coordinate volunteers and a willing business school partner, almost any city can produce the volunteers to replicate UEI. Groups of successful entrepreneurs can mentor fellow entrepreneurs in their community. Small businesses are vital to the fabric of low-income neighborhoods. With just a little of the help large corporations pay handsomely for every year, many more would survive, prosper, keep employees working, hire more people, and strengthen their communities.

ONE EXAMPLE OF MODEL GIVING that has been particularly successful in New York involves churches establishing their own corporations to promote economic development and affordable housing in their communities. The Greater Allen A.M.E. Cathedral, pastored by Revs. Floyd and Elaine Flake, is an African Methodist Episcopal "mega-church" in Jamaica, Queens, with twenty thousand members. Its Preservation and Development Corporation supports commercial development, homeownership, repair and renovation, and foreclosure avoidance. When I first visited the church in 1992, at its previous location, I noticed that it was surrounded by successful small businesses. Most of them had received financing from the church's development arm.

The Abyssinian Baptist Church, a Harlem landmark pastored by Rev. Calvin Butts, also has a development corporation devoted to increasing affordable housing, economic development, and family support. In New York City about 30 percent of the people own their own homes. In central Harlem, the ownership rate is only 13.8 percent. The Abyssinian Development Corporation has created more than one thousand units of affordable housing in eighty-two buildings, most of which have gone to low-income families, the homeless, and senior citizens. In addition, ADC has given more than one hundred moderate-income families the chance to own their own homes and will develop three hundred more over the next three years. ADC has also developed job creation projects, including a Pathmark grocery store and a mixed-use retail and office building that produced a combined seven hundred jobs for local residents.

African-American ministers are stimulating this kind of development all over America, but there's no reason other churches, synagogues, mosques, and temples can't do the same thing.

The most comprehensive American model for citizen service I've come across also centers on African Americans, but can be adopted by others. In February 2006, Tavis Smiley, the prominent African-American radio and television journalist, published *The Covenant with Black America*, a remarkable book analyzing the continuing racial disparities in American life and providing a plan of action for dealing with them in the form of ten "covenants." Each chapter of the book calls on its readers to make a covenant to do something about a particular problem: health care; education; criminal justice; accountable policing; affordable housing in stable neighborhoods; voting rights; rural development; access to jobs and capital; environmental justice; and the racial digital divide. Each chapter opens with a short introductory essay by an expert, followed by a comprehensive list of salient facts and by specific examples of "what the community can do," then "what every individual can do now," "what works now," and "what every leader and elected official can do."

The Covenant touched a nerve with African Americans and others concerned about the future of black America. Within a month of its release, it reached number one on several best-seller lists. All over America, churches, community organizations, civic groups, elected officials, and concerned citizens gathered to discuss how they could become advocates for and agents of change. The response was so great and so rapid that within a year Tavis Smiley published a second book, *The Covenant in Action*, which describes efforts already under way to advance the covenant's goals; profiles young emerging black activists; and provides a toolkit to help readers take on each challenge in a systematic way through political action, legal action, and NGO projects. *The Covenant in Action* is a practical guide to getting involved.

In this short summary, I can't begin to do justice to The Covenant movement, to the power of its inspiration, instruction, and examples. Both of Smiley's books can be read quickly, and the actions they propose can keep you busy for a lifetime. I recommend both books to you because I believe Smiley has given us a model for how to organize other groups with common challenges for action in America and across the world. If you read them, I'm sure you'll agree.

An education program serving minority students that could be replicated in virtually every community is College Track, which works to help low-income students prepare for, get into, and succeed in higher education. Currently, College Track is serving nearly 300 high school and college students at its centers in East Palo Alto and Oakland, California. It provides a summer high school preparation program, workshops, tutoring, and college entrance exam preparation classes; required extracurricular and community service participation; paid summer internships; assistance getting college scholarships and financial aid; and ongoing support in college. College Track is getting results. Nationwide, 29 percent of students from low-income households finish college, but 86 percent of College Track's students will do so. Why does it work? Founder Laurene Powell Jobs says: "Some organizations work to fix the education system through political and policy changes. We don't. At College Track, we focus on kids."

America's Promise, founded by General Colin L. Powell (U.S. Ret.) and his wife, Alma, offers an interesting model for people seeking to advance a cause with multiple programs in which many people are already involved. The mission of America's Promise is to give all children what they need to succeed by keeping five promises to them: the involvement of caring adults, access to safe places, a healthy start, a good education, and opportunities to help others. In its eleventh year, America's Promise has alliances with more than 105 partners from business, NGOs, communities, and policy-makers. Its goal is to deliver more promises to 15 million disadvantaged young people over the next five years.

AMERICA IS BLESSED in having citizens whose roots are in every other nation. Many, perhaps most, of these citizens who have done well have given back not only to their local community but also to their home countries. When they join forces with others who share their heritage they can increase their impact dramatically. I had a chance to see such an effort get off the ground among Indian Americans in the aftermath of the devastating earthquake that brought death and destruction to the western Indian province of Gujarat in 2001.

When I called then prime minister Atal Bihari Vajpayee to see if I could help, he said the government could rebuild the larger areas but needed support for reconstruction of hundreds of smaller villages. I knew that many Indian Americans were already contributing individually to their native land, usually by building hospitals, clinics, and schools and providing scholarships for worthy students. After the earthquake many others were eager to join in. Soon the American India Foundation was born, with a board of directors chaired by Rajat Gupta, senior partner of McKinsey and Company, and Victor Menezes, now retired senior vice chairman of Citigroup. The president is Lata Krishnan, an information technology entrepreneur from Northern California.

The AIF quickly raised more than $4 million for relief, reconstruction, and rehabilitation. In the relief phase, AIF worked through local and international NGOs to provide food, water, and shelter in hundreds of villages, along with 1,200 wheelchairs to permanently disabled victims. Then AIF funds rebuilt more than 1,350 homes, 180 work sheds for thousands of Gujarati artisans skilled in metal, wood, and fine clothing work, dozens of schools and classrooms, three hospitals, and a primary health center. The foundation also provided the funds to finish reconstruction of the embankment of Hamirsar Lake, in the city of Bhuj. The lake is the city's main rainwater collection reservoir, and the damage to the embankment had caused severe flooding that affected 100,000 of the city's residents. In the rehabilitation phase, AIF increased the availability of microcredit loans, training and skills development for women entrepreneurs, and support for people working on farms, in salt mines, and in poor urban areas.

The success in Gujarat convinced the AIF leaders to continue their work. They have now raised more than $37 million from thousands of donors, the vast majority of them Indian Americans. Their funds have been distributed to sixty Indian NGOs working on education, HIV/AIDS, and women's empowerment. AIF's League of Artisans helps develop business opportunities through improved production and marketing. The AIF Digital Equalizer Program has made information technology available to more than 200,000 students. And 140 AIF Indian-American Service Fellows have gone to India to serve for ten months with local NGOs.

I have told the AIF story at some length because America has immigrants from more than 180 other nations, many of them with needs similar to India's. If groups of successful immigrants organized and acted in the same way, it would help an enormous number of people and show America's best face to the world.

IN 2003, MAYA AMOILS, a high school student from Cincinnati, Ohio, demonstrated the potential young people have to create model gifts. Maya is a native of South Africa, and her aunt and uncle own a resort in the mountainous Drakensberg region. Through her aunt and uncle, Maya heard of the plight of the nearby village of Langkloof: its three thousand inhabitants have no running water or sewage system or medical care, and many children have been orphaned by AIDS. Maya and six of her friends established H.O.P.E. (Help Other People Endure), a charity through which kids help kids. The girls sold T-shirts at their school and raised $2,000, which Maya took to Langkloof in 2004 along with toys and clothes they had collected. The money, along with a contribution from her aunt and uncle, was used to start a feeding program to guarantee twelve orphaned children one good meal a day.

In 2005, the girls set a goal of raising $5,000. The publicity and enthusiasm their efforts inspired enabled them to surpass the goal by $145,000, and by May 2007 they had raised a total of $800,000. The feeding program grew to 350 children a day. Eleven teenage H.O.P.E. members traveled to Langkloof to meet with tribal elders and community members, work with the children, renovate a preschool, install a playground, and plant fruit trees and a vegetable garden to provide produce to feed the children.

H.O.P.E. has now expanded to include children from other schools. It is going to construct a community center with running water, flush toilets, and a modern kitchen, build a chicken coop to provide chickens and eggs for the feeding program, develop a working farm with an irrigation system to employ 125 members of the local community, and continue the yearly trips so that H.O.P.E. members can promote education, AIDS prevention, and inspire children to break the cycle of poverty and disease. To achieve these goals, the kids have to raise $300,000. After that, they intend to start adult education classes, scholarships and financial aid for good students, medical services—and to replicate their project in nearby communities. I wouldn't bet against their success.

Could H.O.P.E. provide a model for young people in every community to start their own group to help other kids at home as well as in other countries? Why not? Think of all the exciting things that creative teenagers could do if every high school had its own NGO.

NINE

Giving to Good Ideas

———

T HE WORLD IS full of people with innovative ideas who are willing to give their all to implementing them but don't have money to get started. These "social entrepreneurs" can change the lives of millions of people for the better if only they are helped to follow through on their ideas.

The movement to identify and fund social entrepreneurs in a systematic way, indeed the very term "social entrepreneurship," was the brainchild of one man. Like many of the world's greatest givers, Bill Drayton is not well known outside the global NGO community. But to those who believe in the power of private citizens to improve society, Drayton is a hero. After graduating from Harvard College and Yale Law School and studying economics at Oxford, he worked in management consulting at McKinsey & Company for ten years, then at the Environmental Protection Agency during the Carter administration. At the EPA, Drayton pioneered the notion that business had to be made a partner in protecting the environment through market-based incentives like

emissions trading and replacing regulations that microman-
age business decisions with overall pollution targets that let
businesses determine the most cost-effective way of meeting
them. In 1980, he founded an organization to promote social
and economic innovation and called it Ashoka, after the
third-century B.C. Indian emperor who unified most of
South Asia with his humane, progressive policies. In San-
skrit, "ashoka" means the "active absence of sorrow." The
organization's logo is the oak tree—a symbol of strength and
health—which, as we all know, grows from a tiny acorn.

For years Drayton had been talking to friends and colleagues and traveling the world trying to determine whether
it was possible to identify powerful new ideas for systematic
change and excellent social entrepreneurs capable of implementing them before the viability of the idea or the entrepreneur had been proven. He became convinced that it
could be done and that he should spend his life doing it.
Ashoka began its operations in India with just $50,000 of his
own money and money he raised from friends.

One of the first Ashoka fellows was Gloria de Souza, a
Bombay teacher who believed from her own experience that
old-fashioned, passive rote learning was boring and ineffec-
tive with most students. She used the environment to teach
children to learn by doing, to think rather than memorize, to
problem-solve rather than to repeat. She made learning
active, creative, and fun. De Souza had a burning desire to
see her approach adopted across India. Ashoka believed in
her approach and in her ability to sell it and in 1981 gave her
a four-year grant to cover living expenses so that she could
pursue it. By 1985, she had persuaded Bombay's school
board to introduce environmental studies with her learning
methods into 1,700 schools. Within three years, nearly a
million students were learning her way. By the end of the

decade, the Indian government had made de Souza's environmental studies program part of the official curriculum in the first three grades. An independent evaluation showed that students learning by de Souza's method scored twice as high on reading tests as those who were taught by rote, and mastered writing and mathematics three times as fast. Gloria de Souza was Ashoka's first acorn.

By 2006, Ashoka's budget had grown from $50,000 to $30 million, its fellows from one to more than 1,800 in more than sixty countries on five continents. They have done amazing things in health care, education, economic development, and in advancing equality and social justice. They were all selected through a rigorous process that was based on the potential of their ideas to have national impact, their entrepreneurial capacity to implement and sell them, their persistence in staying the course and making appropriate changes when their plans didn't work out, and their willingness to keep at it for as long as it takes to succeed.

Ashoka tripled in size from 1999 to 2002 and is still growing and expanding its mission. Besides supporting social entrepreneurs, Ashoka now develops groups and networks of them to reinforce each other and accelerate their impact, and it provides infrastructure support, including access to financing for expansion, ties to the business and academic sectors, and opportunities for partnerships with others doing compatible work. At the 2006 Clinton Global Initiative, Ashoka committed to raise $50 million to expand its search for social entrepreneurs in Western Europe, Africa, East Asia, and the Middle East.

Bill Drayton looks more like a college professor than a world-beater. He is modest, very thin, wears old-fashioned big-framed glasses, talks softly, and is polite, almost courtly in manner. He is brilliant, with a wide knowledge of topics both prominent and obscure. I ran into him not long ago at an event in Washington and was struck, as always, by the unusual combination of power, kindness, and humility he projects. A quiet man who set out to change the world by giving citizens in every nation "the freedom, confidence, and social support to address any social need," he is still at it, the perfect model for all the other social entrepreneurs he finds and empowers, and many others he's never met. Bill Drayton's story and those of other promising social entrepreneurs, including some outstanding Ashoka fellows, are told at greater length in David Bornstein's fine book *How to Change the World*. If you're particularly interested in this kind of giving, I highly recommend it.

In recent years, more funding for social entrepreneurs has become available, principally from foundations established by wealthy individuals. Among the most important is the Omidyar Network, established by eBay founder Pierre Omidyar and his wife, Pam. The network funds a broad array of projects that promote empowerment through innovation. It has been a generous supporter of Ashoka and of the Microcredit Summit campaign, an annual meeting of stakeholders that, for a decade now, has focused on reaching the world's poorest families (those living on less than $1 a day), empowering women, building microcredit institutions that are financially self-sufficient, and measuring the impact of microcredit on clients and their families. The summit brings together lenders, advocates, government and NGO donors, educators, and international financial institutions to share best practices and help each other succeed.

The Omidyar Network has funded dozens of other social entrepreneurs across a wide range of activities, including Cell Bazaar, which connects buyers and sellers through a mobile phone–based marketplace; CircleLending, which manages loans between relatives, friends, and other private parties; Common Sense Media, which works to improve the impact of media and entertainment on kids and families; KaBOOM!, a partner in my foundation's efforts against childhood obesity, which helps communities to design, build, and maintain their own playgrounds; and Modest Needs, which helps keep struggling families from falling into poverty by allowing them to cover small but unexpected expenses by pooling what they can afford to share.

Another Omidyar Network recipient, GlobalGiving, also helps to fund social entrepreneurs. Launched in 2002 by two former World Bank executives, Global Giving's Web site, GlobalGiving.com, allows donors at all levels to look through a large list of projects, organized by geography or subject matter. Once a donor locates a project, he or she can contribute any amount, knowing that the donation is tax deductible under U.S. law, that it will reach the project within a month, and that all donors receive regular progress reports on the projects they support.

The Web site offers more than four hundred projects in more than sixty countries. Since 2001, about 750 projects have received over $5 million from more than two thousand donors.

Other foundations set up to fund social entrepreneurs include Echoing Green and the Schwab Foundation for Social Entrepreneurship. Echoing Green, similar to the Ashoka model, was founded in 1987 by American investor Ed Cohen and has provided seed capital to more than 400 social entrepreneurs. The Schwab Foundation was started by Klaus Schwab (who also founded the World Economic Forum) and his wife, Hilde. It has supported more than one hundred entrepreneurs and, at the World Economic Forum's annual meeting in Davos, Switzerland, gives them the opportunity to discuss their work with and garner support from business and foundation executives, prominent government leaders, and heads of multinational agencies.

Long-established foundations are also now more inclined to fund innovation, especially in its early stages. In 2000, the Ford and Annie E. Casey foundations helped launch One Economy, which is committed to bringing broadband into the homes of low-income people and to providing easy-to-access information on education, health, employment, and available public benefits through its multilingual portal, the Beehive (thebeehive.org). There is also a program to help people buy computers. More than 200,000 people have obtained broadband at home thanks to One Economy, and more than 9.5 million people have used the Beehive, nearly two million of them in Spanish.

One Economy began in Washington, D.C., when Rey Ramsey, now its CEO, and three other young people imagined a world with no digital divide, one in which all people could share the benefits of information technology. Now One Economy has programs in a dozen U.S. cities and in South Africa, Mozambique, Jordan, and Egypt. In the United States, it is also working to change housing policies so that broadband is financed as part of the construction of all government-subsidized housing, with remaining costs financed through operating budgets, like security or landscaping. So far One Economy has helped to win policy changes in forty-two states and several cities and counties.

People have used the Beehive to learn about and file for the earned income tax credit; to produce business plans or find jobs; to learn how to create a family budget or how to write a check; to learn how to earn their GED or to access Medicaid benefits; and to get information on health problems, from diabetes to alcoholism. More than forty thousand kids a month use Beehive for homework help, and hundreds of young people have been trained to be Digital Connectors, to help families in their communities learn how to use the Beehive.

One of the most promising examples of multifaceted social entrepreneurship I've witnessed in America is the Harlem Children's Zone, which helps parents, teachers, residents, and other interested parties create a safe learning environment for young people in a sixty-block area of central Harlem, where more than half of the children live below the poverty line and two-thirds of them score below grade level on state reading and math tests. The Zone offers continuous, comprehensive support for children's development, from the time their mothers are pregnant until they go to college or to work. There are workshops for expectant parents and parents of children three and under, a preschool program open to four-year-olds, after-school and summer school programs for students in the five elementary schools in the Harlem Children's Zone, and a chess program. In 2004, the team from Public School 242 tied for fourth place in the national championships. A job center offers young people, ages fourteen to eighteen, year-round training, internships, summer jobs, academic support, and job placement. The Zone's TRUCE program helps high school seniors graduate on time and get into college. They do so at a higher rate than the New York City average. Computer classes and employment help are available to both young people and adults.

The Zone also runs community development programs: a fitness and nutrition center, neighborhood beautification, intergenerational learning, and housing improvement efforts; an asthma initiative (almost one-third of the children in the Zone have asthma, five times the national average); and a young investors program to encourage low-income working families to begin saving for their children's college education while the kids are still in preschool. All told, in 2006, the Zone's fifteen centers served more than 14,400 people, including 9,500 children. Harlem Children's Zone also supports the conversion of public schools in the Zone into charter schools that pay teachers more to keep the schools open longer hours and operate year-round learning programs.

The driving force behind Harlem Children's Zone is its charismatic, visionary president, Geoff Canada. He's taken on a lot of tough challenges at once, convinced that only a comprehensive approach to community building will give all the Zone's children the future they deserve. As the *New York Times Magazine* reported in its June 2004 article on him, Canada asked, "Instead of helping some kids beat the odds, why don't we just change the odds?" Canada's approach is both liberal and conservative. He wants to properly fund programs that work *and* improve parenting and the community culture. He pursues both objectives with the same discipline that earned him a third-degree black belt in the martial art of tae kwon do. What is unique about Canada's approach is not the novelty of his individual programs but their comprehensive sweep. He wants to create a system within which poor children can learn and perform as well as middle-class kids. In a few years we'll know whether Canada's sweeping approach works; whether through programs and services that cost about $1,400 per child, poor children can score at or above grade levels on standardized tests, graduate from school on time, and go on to productive lives in college or in the workforce.

Luckily, there are people willing to provide long-term funding for the Harlem Children's Zone, especially board chairman Stan Druckenmiller, who made his fortune as a hedge fund manager and has devoted himself to the Harlem Children's Zone with the same zeal and intelligence that made him a success in the stock market. Druckenmiller and the other board members contribute about a third of the annual operating budget. The rest comes from foundations, other private donors, and public funds.

There are worthy, if less comprehensive, ideas in every community that need support to come to life. One of the things our staff at the Clinton Global Initiative tries to do is match social entrepreneurs with potential donors. One such match was made between Sustainable South Bronx, an NGO managed by Majora Carter, and Barry Segal, CEO of Bradco Supply, a New Jersey roofing company.

The South Bronx includes the poorest congressional district in the United States. More than 40 percent of its population lives at or below the poverty line. Its unemployment rate is around 25 percent, more than three times the New York City average. It is two-thirds Hispanic, one-third African American. The obesity rate is 27 percent, the asthma hospitalization rate seven times the national average. The area has a core residential section surrounded by manufacturing facilities, utilities, and warehouses. It has the least amount of green open space in the city, less than one-half acre per thousand people.

Carter won a federal grant to design the South Bronx Greenway, an eleven-mile bicycle and pedestrian path connecting neighborhoods to the waterfront, and for a new park to be constructed there. The city government committed the money necessary to build the greenway and the park, but did not commit to fund a maintenance plan. So Majora came up with the idea of creating South Bronx Greenway Stewards to protect the community investment in green space and to provide young residents with jobs, leadership training, and educational programs. Then at the 2006 Clinton Global Initiative, she met Barry Segal, who became her first big partner, with a $100,000 donation. If you're interested, Sustainable South Bronx needs more support, as do other places all over America and throughout the world that would benefit from more urban parkland and forests.

Majora Carter is a charismatic, energetic, highly intelligent woman with a graduate degree in English literature. When I asked her how she decided to set up Sustainable South Bronx and devote her life to it, she told me she grew up in the South Bronx, and a few years ago, when she started graduate school, she moved back in with her parents. She said, "I discovered the old neighborhood wasn't as bad as I thought, but people had given up. There were too many toxic facilities—four power plants and dumps with 40 percent of New York's garbage." Carter organized a drive to beat back another waste facility, started a job-training program for waste clean-up, and set up Sustainable South Bronx to create more jobs by improving the environment. She's hoping to get in on the ground floor of Mayor Bloomberg's ambitious plan to reduce New York City's greenhouse gas emissions. Why does she keep at it? "Because I see changes. People feel different when there's beauty. They know someone cares. It's intoxicating to me." Majora recently married, and her husband, a filmmaker, left his work and joined her at Sustainable South Bronx. They live across the street from where she grew up. If your area needs more green space, Majora could give you some ideas about how to get started.

Great ideas that merit support can arise from unpredictable circumstances. Tragedies have produced some remarkable initiatives funded by people who lost someone they cared about, and others sympathetic to their cause. The

Rory Peck Trust, a British NGO, funds training for journalists going into dangerous areas with a special program named for Richard Wild, a reporter killed on the job in Iraq. After Daniel Pearl was murdered by terrorists in Pakistan, his family, friends, and colleagues set up a foundation and scholarship in his name to allow aspiring journalists to pursue their careers. When brilliant young British lawyer Nick Weber was killed in a car crash in Malawi where he was providing legal services to poor people, a trust set up in his name established a law library and provided scholarships to law students who agreed to follow Nick's example in providing legal aid after graduating.

A few years ago, I had the opportunity to see a great idea born out of tragedy come to life. On May 28, 2001, I was in the north of Scotland, having finished a respectable round of golf on the Old Course at St. Andrews—the dream of every avid golfer. I had just checked into my room and was looking forward to a leisurely dinner and another round of golf the next day. Then the phone rang. It was my office calling to tell me that the daughter of my closest childhood friend, David Leopoulos, had been killed in a car accident in Little Rock.

It was heartbreaking. Thea Leopoulos was just seventeen, a good student, a gifted artist essentially self-taught, a beautiful girl inside and out, so beloved by her fellow students that two thousand people attended her memorial service. I loved her too. When I left Arkansas for the White House, I had a special zip code established for my personal friends so their letters wouldn't get lost in the crush of mail. Thea wrote me often, and through her letters I saw her growing up into a young woman of great faith and generous spirit, wise beyond her years. Some of her best letters came in times of trouble. They were always full of love, affection, and keen observations on current events from her often humorous perspective.

David and his wife, Linda, were devastated by their daughter's death, as were her brothers, Thaddeus and Nick. But they were also moved by the seemingly endless accounts of Thea's kindness and good deeds not just from her fellow students but from their parents as well. They decided to set up a foundation in Thea's name to focus on strengthening families and supporting the arts. Andy Manatos, a Washington, D.C., lawyer David had gotten to know working on issues of interest to Greek Americans, helped him get the organization started, and the first board members included longtime friends like Mauria Aspell, a gifted social worker, our grade school classmate Rose Crane, who does much of the strategic planning, and me.

The THEA Foundation held a few successful family conferences but soon decided to focus exclusively on the arts, especially on preserving arts programs in the schools and giving arts scholarships to help more young people go on to college. David gave up his career and went to work full-time on the foundation. In 2002, the THEA Foundation gave its first three performing arts scholarships worth $1,700. By 2006, it was giving away twenty scholarships worth $266,000. So far, fifty-five winners of visual and performing arts contests have won scholarships worth $600,000: $100,000 from the foundation, $500,000 from Arkansas colleges and universities and THEA business partners.

THEA also sponsors acting and dance workshops for hundreds of students featuring Arkansas natives Mary Steenburgen (and her husband, Ted Danson), Harry Thomason, Lawrence Hamilton, and Elizabeth Williams; teacher workshops, helping 1,500 teachers deal with kids with personal and/or learning problems; THEA's Art Closet, offering free art supplies and materials to public school teachers who otherwise would have to pay for them out of their own pocket; and Art Across Arkansas, which has helped place a piece of fine art in sixty-eight public schools this year and will do so in another 150 schools next year. So far, almost fifty artists have made permanent donations of their work to Art Across Arkansas.

I believe the THEA Foundation will spark a revival of arts education in my native state. Just as with music in the schools, exposure to and involvement with fine arts aids the learning process in other areas, improving self-confidence, concentration, problem solving, and academic performance. Painting changed Thea Leopoulos's life. She became a better, more self-assured student, and she produced some remarkable pieces.

The worst fate that can befall a parent turned my friend into a great social entrepreneur. For the past five years, he's funded THEA's operations and scholarship portions mostly out of the proceeds from an annual benefit, hosted by Andy Manatos in Washington, and contributions from me, but its donor base is expanding as it becomes better known. In 2007, most of Arkansas's institutions of higher education and thirty-four businesses are putting up scholarship money.

I have written about the THEA foundation at some length because it's a model that can be expanded or replicated across the country, wherever arts education has been given short shrift, and I hope we can generate the interest and get the backing to do it. I've also highlighted THEA because it provides further evidence that passionate, innovative people with the power to change many lives are everywhere. David Leopoulos has brought great honor to his daughter's memory and kept her spirit alive in the eyes of young people discovering the arts for the first time.

Most communities have people who want to pursue noble goals. Maybe you're one of them. If you are, I hope David's example will give you the confidence to try. If you're willing to support someone like him, be on the lookout: he or she may live next door.

You may be reading this and thinking, "Well, I have a great giving idea, but I don't have a friend who was president or who's a successful Washington lawyer. What can I do?" Here's a story anyone with energy, imagination, and commitment can emulate.

Twenty-five years ago Edward and Maya Manley's daughter, then just fourteen, developed a brain tumor. Surgery and chemotherapy proved effective, and she went on to lead a full life. But their struggle left the Manleys with a desire to do something to help families in the same situation. At first they tried raising funds to support more brain tumor research, but after a few years they decided what they really wanted to do was to create a support network for the families. In September 1996, along with Clint Greenbaum, another parent of a survivor, they founded the Making Headway Foundation, to help children with brain and spinal cord tumors. Starting small and growing to meet the demand for its work, Headway now provides support for children and their families before, during, and after hospital care, including free counseling, support groups, and, when surgery, radiation, and chemotherapy have caused learning disabilities, education remediation services. When the children don't survive, Making Headway offers support to the families, including assistance when needed in paying for funeral expenses.

Hillary and I met the Manleys when we moved to Chappaqua. They live about two miles from us, and we always try to attend the Family Fun Day they host every June in their backyard for about four hundred people. Brave families with kids who want to laugh again and friends of the foundation enjoy games, a show, a petting zoo, and great barbecue.

How do the Manleys cover the foundation's budget, which has grown to more than $800,000 a year? Though they welcome contributions on their Web site and receive donations through the United Way, they raise most of their funds in small amounts from people at events, including a "walk by the water" at Point Lookout, New York, two golf tournaments, a dinner dance, and a concert. In January 2007, they sold tickets at $75 and $100 to a performance by Strawberry Fields, a delightful Beatles tribute band. The foundation also solicits toys and games for young patients and their siblings during the hospital stay and has recently established a medical research fund to which donors can direct their gifts. Making Headway is as excellent model for putting a good idea into action by asking for help from friends, family, neighbors, and those who share a passion for the cause. It's something you could do.

TEN

Organizing Markets for the Public Good

———

O NE OF THE most interesting things I've learned since leaving the presidency and entering the NGO and business worlds is how many markets for "public goods"—from lifesaving medications to clean energy products and energy-efficient practices—are disorganized and unnecessarily small. There are enormous opportunities for businesses to increase profits, and for NGOs to make contributors' money go further, by organizing and enlarging such markets. Though we may not think of it as giving in the usual sense, organizing and enlarging public goods markets are important ways of giving that can both benefit and involve millions of people in advancing good causes. I want to discuss these markets at some length, because they also create real opportunities for each of us to be more effective givers of our time and money by simply changing our buying habits as ordinary consumers. When we support companies that do good things, the increased demand will cause other companies to follow suit.

The problem of climate change presents an existential

threat to the future of civilization. Global warming is caused by increased concentrations of greenhouse gases, principally carbon dioxide and methane. Scientists believe CO_2 levels are higher than they have been in 650,000 years. Glaciers and snowcaps are melting all over the world. Severe weather events are increasing. The composition of the oceans is changing, threatening coral reefs and further eroding fish stocks. Diseases once confined to tropical climates are spreading to new areas as the weather warms. Sea levels are rising, threatening to flood coastal areas and displace tens of millions before the century is out. The scientific consensus that climate change is real and caused by man-made activities is overwhelming. The only debate is over how soon really bad things will happen and how bad they will be.

Most man-made CO_2 emissions come from burning oil and coal. Most methane emissions caused by humans come from landfills and agriculture, though increasingly methane is being released from long-frozen tundra as a result of global warming. The big increase in emissions began with the discovery of oil and the Industrial Revolution's need for oil and coal, with most of the emissions occurring in the last fifty or so years, as more nations industrialized and the global population increased dramatically.

Though India and China will soon surpass us, the United States is now the largest emitter of greenhouse gases. With 5 percent of the world's population and 21 percent of its economic output, Americans account for 25 percent of the emissions. So far, our nation has refused to take serious action on climate change for four reasons: 1) though it is no longer true, too many people still believe a nation cannot become wealthy and stay that way without burning more coal and oil; 2) the old energy economy, rooted in oil and coal, is well organized, well financed, and well connected politically, while the new energy economy is decentralized, disorganized, undercapitalized, and less influential; 3) until recently, oil was too cheap to encourage clean alternatives and conservation, and even today, it is not generally accepted that oil is a depleting resource that experts believe will be used up sometime within fifty to a hundred years; and 4) so far, too many politicians have been resistant to implementing proven strategies to reduce emissions, like emission-trading schemes, high efficiency standards for appliances, lighting, buildings, and automobiles, and comprehensive efforts to maximize the use of clean energy sources.

Al Gore has been warning us of the dangers of climate change for more than twenty years. His landmark book, *Earth in the Balance*, made a deep impression on me and was one of the reasons I asked him to be my running mate in 1992. When Al won an Academy Award for his fine documentary, *An Inconvenient Truth*, I was thrilled. America was finally listening to the lecture he'd given me every week for eight years!

In 1993, my first year as president, we included as part of the Deficit Reduction Act a small carbon tax that would have led to more conservation. We convinced the House to pass it, but it died in the Senate. After that, we pursued a partnership with the U.S. automakers to develop a very high-mileage car, took steps to increase energy efficiency in the federal government, which had the effect of taking several hundred thousand cars off the road, increased research, and negotiated the Kyoto Climate Change Treaty to howls that it would destroy the economy. Virtually the entire Senate voted for a resolution opposing the treaty even before I could submit it for ratification. In my second term, I gave what I thought was a compelling speech about climate change, which elicited a giant yawn among all but the most well-informed members of the press. Of course, it didn't help that at the time the price of oil was below $30 a barrel and the economy was booming.

All that changed after 9/11 and the Iraq War. With oil prices soaring and mounting evidence of the destructive impacts of climate change, everyone began to take the issue more seriously. Senator John McCain and Hillary led delegations of more skeptical senators to northern Norway and Alaska to see the already clear impact of warming for themselves. Other countries proved that clean efficient energy use could be profitable. Denmark increased the size of its economy 50 percent with *no* increase in energy use and a reduction in greenhouse gas emissions, in part by generating more than 20 percent of its electricity from wind, the highest percentage in the world. While the U.S. government was condemning Kyoto as a threat to growth, the United Kingdom determined to beat its Kyoto reduction target by 25 to 50 percent, and in so doing created enough good jobs to enjoy something we Americans didn't—rising wages and declining inequality. Germany is now the number one producer of wind energy, and Japan leads the world in the production and installation of solar panels.

We could accomplish all that here. California, which has been working on energy conservation seriously for more than thirty years, has a per capita energy use that is only 50 percent of the U.S. average. To date, the U.S. government's positive actions have been confined to a modest increase in research and development and in tax incentives for purchasing clean energy products, incentives that still are not nearly as great as those that remain available to the old energy economy, or as those producing a boom in solar and wind energy in Japan, Germany, and Spain. The most encouraging development in America is the blizzard of activity being undertaken by the private sector and by individual communities and states.

With evidence of climate change clear and oil costing more than $60 a barrel, there are almost limitless opportunities to make money out of doing the right thing. The biofuel industry is exploding, bringing with it a potential revival in the fortunes of rural America. Most American companies are far ahead of the government in seeing the climate change problem as an economic opportunity. Those that are leading the way are giving you the chance to do something about climate change too, by supporting them with your purchasing power.

Wal-Mart is one of the world's largest companies, with 1.8 million employees and revenues of over $315 billion. Every week 176 million customers shop at Wal-Marts in fourteen countries. It has more than sixty thousand suppliers worldwide and stocks 142,000 items in a typical U.S. Supercenter. Wal-Mart's president, Lee Scott, is a straight-talking Midwesterner whose unfailingly calm demeanor and soft voice can be deceptive. He has a quick mind, a good imagination, and a wry sense of humor. A couple of years ago, I had an interesting conversation with him at a time when Wal-Mart was being heavily criticized for everything from its employment and employee benefit practices, to its huge volume of imports from China, to the pressure it puts on smaller competitors. We talked about the need to do more on climate change. For several years, Wal-Mart had been actively pursuing energy conservation to reduce costs, and I pointed out that most of its customers were people of modest income who would also save money if the company adopted a much more comprehensive effort that involved them.

A little more than a year later, Wal-Mart announced its

Sustainability 360 plan. With input from several environmental and energy experts, Wal-Mart devised a strategy to pursue three ambitious goals: to be supplied 100 percent by renewable energy; to create zero waste; and to sell sustainable products that conserve resources and protect the environment.

They're off to a good start, with a new prototype store that uses 20 percent less energy and reduced packaging on a line of toys that will require 497 fewer containers to ship, saving $2.4 million in annual shipping costs, 3,800 trees, and 1,000 barrels of oil. In six years, the company will reduce packaging by 5 percent, removing 213,000 trucks from the road, saving 324,000 tons of coal and 67 million gallons of diesel fuel a year, and cutting costs throughout its supply chain by about $3.4 billion. In the United Kingdom, Wal-Mart will reduce food packaging by 25 percent next year and will send *no* waste to landfills by 2010. All told, Wal-Mart estimates that its packaging reductions will reduce CO_2 emissions by 667,000 metric tons by 2013. In addition, Wal-Mart has partnered with GE to develop highly efficient LED (light-emitting diode) lighting for its refrigerator cases, saving $13 million and 63 million pounds of CO_2 emissions a year.

To get its customers involved in reducing emissions, the company is trying to sell 100 million compact fluorescent lightbulbs in the United States by the end of this year. They cost three times as much but last five to ten times as long as the more common incandescent bulbs and use so much less energy (about one-fourth as much to produce the same light) that, even with the higher purchase price, a consumer will realize a 25 to 40 percent savings in electric bills each year. If every household in the United States replaces one bulb with a compact fluorescent bulb, they'll help keep 9 billion tons of carbon dioxide out of the air, the equivalent of taking 800,000 cars off the road. Many consumers resist using the compact fluorescent bulbs because they don't seem as bright and some have a short delay before turning on, but they're getting better all the time. If you support the stores that sell them and the companies that make them, you'll save money on your electric bill and encourage lower prices and more products that use even less electricity. For example, I just bought a 6-watt LED desk light that is as bright as a conventional 60-watt bulb.

The nation's second-largest retailer, Home Depot, is also making an aggressive effort to persuade its customers to go green, introducing the Eco Options labeling program for nearly three thousand products that promote energy conservation, clean water, and sustainable forestry. The products include fluorescent lightbulbs, silicon windows, and door sealants that improve the efficiency of heating and cooling systems. They even have a calculator on their Web site so you can evaluate the savings you will generate by switching from incandescent to compact fluorescent lightbulbs. Home Depot plans to have six thousand Eco Options products, representing 12 percent of its sales, by 2009.

Tesco, a large European retailer with operations in Asia, claims to be building "the greenest store in the world," a supermarket made entirely from recyclable materials. All shopping bags will be biodegradable and shoppers will be able to return excess packaging to Tesco stores for recycling. The company has also established an environmental fund of £100 million (almost $200 million) to power its stores with wind turbines, solar panels, and geothermal power.

Many other big companies are making aggressive efforts to promote energy efficiency and clean energy in ways that not only increase profits but raise consumer awareness.

United Technologies Corporation, the twentieth-largest manufacturing corporation in the United States, consumes thirty trillion BTUs of energy a year, and the use of its products account for 2 percent of the world's greenhouse gas emissions. Over the last decade, while enjoying robust growth, it has reduced annual energy consumption by 18 percent. Since 2001, it has reduced greenhouse gas emissions by 16 percent per dollar of revenue. Among United Technologies' most interesting innovations is EcoPower, which cleans its Pratt & Whitney jet engines without using toxic chemicals in a closed-loop process that saves fuel. Hawaiian Airlines estimates that EcoPower will cut its annual fuel use by Boeing 767s by 2.5 million pounds and cut carbon dioxide emissions by nearly 8 million pounds. Imagine the savings if every commercial jet used EcoPower.

United Technologies is not the only big company investing in a clean energy future and betting it will be profitable. Whirlpool, DuPont, and more than forty other companies, including Royal Dutch Shell and British Petroleum, several major utilities, two big forest products corporations, high-tech firms, and engine manufacturers, have been united by the Pew Center on Global Climate Change to lobby the federal government for limits on CO_2 emissions. One of the largest is GE, which, under its new chairman, Jeff Immelt, has decided to join the green revolution and do it in a profitable way.

Most Americans think of GE in terms of consumer products like lightbulbs and appliances, but most of its revenue comes from supplying large equipment to utilities, railroads, other industrial companies, and governments—all large energy users. GE calls its new commitment "ecomagination." Launched in 2005, it includes commitments by GE to reduce greenhouse gas emissions one percent by 2012 through improvements in energy efficiency (they could otherwise have increased by 30 percent due to growth); double annual research in cleaner technologies from $700 million to $1.5 billion by 2010; and double revenues from ecomagination products to $20 billion by 2010.

The research agenda includes the development of more efficient wind energy, including offshore wind turbines; less costly solar panels; a greater variety of biofuels; cost-effective electricity generation from biomass, heat, and geothermal energy; cleaner coal technology that could generate electricity as cleanly as natural gas production and emit only water vapor; advanced fuel cells; commercially viable hydrogen energy; a 30 percent reduction in energy consumption for waste water reuse and recycling; and affordable LED lighting for homes and businesses.

GE has already certified more than forty-five ecomagination products, with more in the pipeline. It is now selling three thousand wind turbines per year, making it the world's second-largest manufacturer of windmills after Denmark's Vestas Wind Systems. It sells an organic waste reuse project that burns waste to generate energy, a Solar Water Filtration system, and the LED lighting Wal-Mart is installing in its refrigeration units. It is also developing cleaner jet engines that use 15 percent less fuel and more fuel-efficient locomotives, which burn 5 percent less fuel and emit 40 percent less pollution. China has already bought three hundred of them and there is a backlog of fifteen hundred more orders from around the world. Locomotives made in Erie, Pennsylvania, are also being sold to Mexico, Brazil, and Kazakhstan because they are the most energy-efficient in the world, costing more in the short run but less over the life of the engine. GE's consumer products include compact fluorescent lightbulbs and energy-efficient washing machines that utilize less water. GE markets its green products with a report card that shows prospective customers exactly how much money and CO_2 they will save from greater efficiency and lower emissions. By its sheer size and serious commitment, GE has the ability to create markets for green products, vastly expanding the potential for greenhouse gas reductions as old technologies are replaced with new ones. GE CEO Jeff Immelt calls the rationale "green is green": that developing advanced, efficient technologies can help cleanse the environment—and the company can make money selling them. As the strategy makes money, its competitors will likely emulate it. What is good for the environment can be good for business.

Across the Pacific, the Japanese electronics giant Sanyo is also remaking itself as a green company. The company has adopted a new philosophy: "Think Gaia" (Gaia was the ancient Greek goddess of the earth). Sanyo's change was part innovation, part necessity, due to competition in conventional consumer electronics from several rivals, particularly Korean firms.

And Sanyo is backing up its commitment with products we can buy. Japan leads the world in the production and installation of photovoltaic solar cells, and Sanyo has long been a global leader in the technology. I first observed the company's widespread use of solar energy when I visited two of its facilities in Japan in 1979. Sanyo's newest solar panels have a cell conversion efficiency of almost 20 percent, perhaps the world's highest, and it is now producing double panels, which also capture solar reflections from the ground, increasing power generation by another 8 percent. In addition, Sanyo has developed an air conditioner, largely for developing countries, which is 99 percent free of chlorofluorocarbon gases; a washing machine that saves energy by using air, not water, to wash clothes; a self-recharging battery for hybrid vehicles (my Mercury SUV hybrid is powered by a Sanyo battery); numerous water conservation technologies that save energy as they conserve and reuse water; and, perhaps most amazing, the eneloop rechargeable battery, which is more powerful and longer lasting than traditional dry cell batteries of the same size and can be recharged one thousand times! More than 22 million eneloops have been delivered in thirty-seven countries. If consumers buy these 22 million batteries and make full use of them, it will reduce the need to dispose of billions of dry cell batteries in the future, and will reduce greenhouse gas emissions from batteries by 98 percent, about the same amount absorbed by all the trees and vegetation in Yosemite National Park. As an added bonus, besides the regular plug-in recharger, there is a recharger that operates on solar power: you just place it in the window. As with compact fluorescent lightbulbs, these batteries and the little time it requires to recharge them will take some getting used to, but Sanyo is giving you another painless way to reduce greenhouse gas emissions.

Swiss Re, the international reinsurance company, has taken a unique approach to involving all its more than ten thousand employees in combating climate change by supporting their efforts to reduce their own emissions. The initiative is titled COyou2—Reduce and Gain. Over the next five years the company will contribute 50 percent of the cost of any employee investment up to 5,000 CHF ($4,000). This will enable the employees in more than twenty-five countries where the company has operations to choose the CO_2 reduction investment most suited to a particular location, from buying hybrid vehicles, to installing solar panels or heat pumps, to improving lighting and insulation. If all its employees cooperate, Swiss Re could invest more than $40 million, creating new markets and better prices for clean energy.

Cisco, the global information technology giant, has committed to reduce its CO_2 emissions by 10 percent, primarily through a 20 percent company-wide travel reduction. It has also made a pledge with potentially far greater impact. The company will invest $15 million over the next three to five years to develop plans to reduce traffic congestion in cities, beginning with San Francisco, Seoul, and Amsterdam. Based on the projects, Cisco will formulate a Connected Urban Development program, which can be used to reduce congestion in other urban areas, lowering CO_2 emissions and saving both citizens and local governments time and money.

At the 2006 Clinton Global Initiative, Sir Richard Branson pledged all future profits of his Virgin Group's airline and rail business, an estimated $3 billion over the next ten years, to investments in renewable energy, and to becoming a carbon-neutral company through greater efficiency in energy use and investments in carbon offset programs. Virgin has already invested in several U.S. ethanol plants, including one in California designed to operate cheaper and greener than standard corn-based plants. Branson is also investing in a bio–diesel fuel for nonelectric trains, and has initiated production of bio–jet fuel, which, if successful, would lead to a huge reduction in greenhouse gas emissions.

Recently, Branson and Al Gore announced the establishment of the Virgin Earth Challenge, which will award a prize of $25 million to the individual or group who is able to demonstrate a commercially viable design in an effort to remove at least a billion tons of greenhouse gases from the atmosphere per year for at least a decade. The prize will be open for five years, with a distinguished panel of judges meeting annually to determine whether a design that offers the promise of such a huge breakthrough has been submitted. There are fascinating possibilities out there. For example, Klaus Lackner, a professor at Columbia University, has designed a synthetic tree to remove carbon dioxide from the atmosphere, a process already in place with more limited technology on nuclear submarines whose crews are sometimes required to spend months in the ocean deeps. At the 2007 World Economic Forum in Davos, one scientist discussed the development of a photoconductive (solar-powered) fiber that presumably could be used in clothes and furniture; another discussed cutting the cost of producing cellulosic ethanol (the amount of energy it takes to produce one gallon of corn-based ethanol is more than five times that of what it takes to produce one gallon of cellulosic ethanol); still another talked about the prospect of genetically modifying viruses to be hybrid materials that can store energy. Such organisms could be used to make batteries, solar cells, and fuel cells. Someone else may have to match Richard Branson's $25 million so there can be more than one prize.

For progress in reducing automobile emissions, there is already another prize. The X PRIZE Foundation, which gave $10 million to the team that built the first private spacecraft to leave the earth's atmosphere, is offering the same amount to anyone who can develop a car that will get 100 miles a gallon *and* can be mass-produced. Several cars getting more than 100 miles a gallon have been made, but so far all have been too costly to be mass-produced. That's the problem the X PRIZE Foundation wants to solve. The prize winner will be selected based on competition races in 2009. If such a car is produced, millions of us will rush to buy it, and transportation-generated CO_2 emissions will plummet.

The move to develop clean energy markets and replicable models that increase profits and reduce greenhouse gases is being driven not just by big companies and prize givers but also by venture capitalists and green social entrepreneurs. Perhaps the most important venture capitalist is Vinod Khosla, a partner in the legendary Silicon Valley venture capital firm of Kleiner Perkins Caufield & Byers. Khosla came to the United States after graduating from the Indian Institute of Technology and found his way to Silicon Valley and an MBA at Stanford. In 1982, he started Sun Microsystems with funding from his friend John Doerr of Kleiner Perkins, another visionary venture capitalist with a strong social conscience. In 2004, Khosla put much of his personal fortune into Khosla Ventures, which invests in both for-profit and "social-impact" projects. He is working with partners to provide microcredit to 25 million borrowers living below the poverty line, to improve health and education in India, and to build a "Global Home" for $5,000. Most important, in terms of market building, he is one of America's foremost advocates of a clean energy future, investing in ethanol and other biofuels, bio-plastics, solar power, and other environmentally friendly technologies. Khosla believes that clean energy entrepreneurs can lift the burden of climate change from our children's future and, in the process, spark an explosion of new businesses and good jobs in the United States, just as information technology did in the 1990s.

Other Silicon Valley entrepreneurs are following Khosla into clean energy, riding the wave of concern about climate change and sensing the evident new economic opportunities in the wake of the collapse of many Internet companies in the first half of the decade. The silicon in computer chips can be used to make solar panels; nanotechnology may be able to cut dramatically the cost of solar energy; and advances in bioengineering may soon make cellulosic ethanol conversion cost-effective. According to Cleantech Venture Network, venture capitalists put more than $400 million into clean energy start-ups in the first three quarters of 2006.

In the United States, we use 70 percent of our oil for transportation. We already know how to replace it all, except for the relatively small portion used for jet fuel. We use the other 30 percent for things like plastics and chemicals, for which there are not viable substitutes. That may be changing too. Cargill is using corn and soybeans as oil substitutes in plastics and chemicals, and its products are finding their way into carpets, disposable cups, plastic bags, Astroturf, lipstick, and the body panels of John Deere combines. If the program continues and consumers and businesses support it, the United States and other nations could become oil-free in a few decades. That would be good for our economy and our security, as well as for the fight against global warming.

Clean energy technologies are catching on outside Europe, Japan, and North America. Brazil pioneered the world's most efficient ethanol from cane sugar and 70 percent of new cars in the country are built to run on it. Prime Minister Meles Zenawi of Ethiopia told me he too wants to produce cane-based ethanol, and believes Africa as a whole should embrace the goal of running all the continent's vehicles on biofuel, reducing harmful emissions (most studies predict Africa will be hardest hit by climate change), and dramatically increasing income among the millions of poor farmers in rural areas. My friend Rolando González-Bunster, a major producer of electricity in the Dominican Republic and other Latin American countries, is in the process of building two wind farms there, with support from donor nations and the International Finance Corporation.

The larger of the two projects will be located in a windy area on the coast near Haiti, with which he hopes to share the power. Because of the international financial support, the electricity can be sold inexpensively and could be particularly helpful to Haiti, which has been virtually denuded—often by poor people scavenging wood for fuel—with disastrous consequences, including loss of topsoil and pollution of fishing sites from runoff. The Solar Electric Light Fund has been providing low-cost solar power for more than twenty years to villages in poor nations not on their nation's power grid. Decentralized power from solar (and wind) may well be the wave of the future, just as cell phones are making telephone lines unnecessary. Saving the planet and saving money can work in developing countries as well as developed ones. We should hope clean energy entrepreneurs succeed everywhere. If they do, all of us, as consumers, will have even more opportunities to do our part.

Amory Lovins has been telling us for more than thirty years that we have opportunities right now. In terms of the scope and detail of his work and his sheer persistence, Lovins is almost certainly the most important clean-energy social entrepreneur of our time. He has never wanted to do anything that doesn't make economic sense, and he has been demonstrating the financial benefits of energy conservation for a long time. Until the last few years, most of what he said was dismissed or ignored by all but the most devoted environmentalists.

I first met Lovins in January 1977, when, as the new attorney general of Arkansas, I asked him to give testimony before our Public Service Commission in opposition to the construction of a large nuclear power plant that would require a substantial increase in consumer utility bills. I didn't know anything about global warming then, I just wanted to hold the rates down and stop wasting so much energy. I had read an essay Lovins published the year before in *Foreign Affairs*, in which he argued that, over a period of decades, America could wean itself off fossil fuels completely and do so not by curtailing economic growth but in a way that would increase it. Lovins helped me argue that Arkansas could meet its future energy needs through greater efficiency at far less cost than the proposed nuclear plant entailed.

Our arguments were treated with curiosity and almost total disbelief. I was only thirty years old, and Amory was a year or so younger. I still had the long hair I'd worn as a law professor, and he looked like a colleague on the science faculty with his thick mustache, unruly hair, and old-fashioned eyeglasses, all three of which he still sports. The conventional, commonsense crowd thought we were both nuts, but I knew he made a lot of sense and understood the details of how energy could be used and consumed better than those who dismissed us. He was also already warning about the potential damage to the climate from increasing CO_2 emissions.

We lost the battle—Amory has lost a lot of them over the years—but finally he may be winning the war for a clean, progressive energy future. Over the years he's produced a flood of books and articles, often filled with mind-numbing technical detail, telling us exactly how to do what most of us now know we have to do. He's also built a home in the Colorado mountains that maximizes conservation and clean energy use. It has no furnace; it's heated by solar panels and heat collected in various parts of the house, including an indoor pond. When I was there a couple of years ago, Amory even had a thriving banana tree. He told me that in the past year the house had been completely self-sufficient; his total electric bill was zero.

Lovins does his work through the Rocky Mountain Institute, a firm he founded twenty-five years ago. Its mission is to use resources in a way that makes the world "secure, just, prosperous, and life-sustaining." His clients have included the Department of Defense; utility, oil, and mining companies; and my presidential library. He helped Wal-Mart develop its plan to double the fuel efficiency of its truck fleet. And he assisted Texas Instruments in the design of a new chip-manufacturing plant in Richardson, Texas. At a time when so many companies say they can't afford to operate in America anymore, Texas Instruments, largely because of energy conservation and cost-effective use of resources, was able to keep in the United States an important plant, which will use 20 percent less energy, 35 percent less water, and cost 30 percent less to build than a chip factory of the same size normally would.

The thing I like best about Amory Lovins is that he's always been in the solutions business. He is relentlessly optimistic and gets the best results possible in every situation. While I was working on this chapter, two of his colleagues visited our home in Chappaqua, New York, to help develop and design a plan to cut the greenhouse gas emissions Hillary and I generate in our more than hundred-year-old farmhouse. More and more people are listening to Lovins, reading his articles, and implementing his practical ideas. Eventually, they'll become part of building codes, utility design and distribution plans, and corporate operations.

Meanwhile, Lovins will keep pushing the envelope. In his recent book *Winning the Oil Endgame*, he argues that we can do without oil imports by 2040, do without oil entirely by 2050, and grow wealthier doing so. He says that for one-fourth the cost of buying it we could eliminate our oil use by switching to ultra-light cars, trucks, and planes (50 percent); substituting advanced biofuels for gasoline and diesel (20 percent); and replacing the rest of the oil with natural gas (30 percent). Where would we get the natural gas? By cutting electricity consumption from inefficient gas-fired power plants, of course. Lovins believes we can do all this without more taxes, legal mandates, the huge up-front shutdown and waste disposal costs of nuclear power, or even more tax incentives. We cannot do it without a much larger, better-organized market for the public goods he advocates. That requires more investment, and greater consumer awareness of what our real options are. If it doesn't happen, it won't be Lovins's fault. If it does, he'll help us give our children a great gift: a more secure, prosperous, sustainable future.

Remember, even if you're acting alone, there's something you can do. After the 2006 Clinton Global Initiative, Amy Oliver e-mailed us to say she would buy energy-efficient lightbulbs and appliances and teach her children to do the same. Jessica wrote that after years of recycling and driving hybrid cars, she intended to take a job working for a sustainable environment. Your ability to contribute may fall somewhere in between. If you want to explore what steps your own community can take to promote clean energy, I recommend *It's Easy Being Green*, by Crissy Trask. In the meantime, at the very least we can all follow Amy Oliver's example.

ENERGY ISN'T THE only area in which the private sector has organized markets for the public good. One of my favorites is the market for fair trade coffee, where companies have joined to ensure that the world's coffee farmers, most of whom are small landowners in developing nations, earn a decent income. The farmers are organized in local cooperatives and all are guaranteed a minimum price of $1.41 per pound regardless of market fluctuations; credit at fair rates; and long-term contracts. The minimum price is very important because the market can drop below $.50 a pound, with no corresponding drop in prices at coffee shops. The companies sign licensing agreements with an organization called TransFair, which monitors the coffee-growing to make sure that fair wages and decent working conditions are maintained and certifies goods with a fair trade label. Among the major fair trade sellers are Equal Exchange, Diedrich, Green Mountain, Peet's, Tully's, and Starbucks. I have personally seen the results of Starbucks's commitment in Rwanda and in Aceh, the Indonesian state devastated by the tsunami. Both places were selected by Starbucks to provide one of the special brews the company features each month. The company sent employees to work with local people to ensure the quality of the coffee beans and production and then marketed the product in an attractive package. In my local coffee shop, both items sold out well before their month was over. Last September a woman e-mailed me to say that from now on she would only buy fair trade coffee. We could all do that by simply buying goods with the fair trade certified label.

In 1999, my administration executed a unique trade agreement with Cambodia that gave U.S. clothing companies the opportunity to be fair trade purchasers. We promised greater access to the U.S. market if the Cambodian factories applied both local labor laws and international labor standards, including a ban on forced labor and child labor—a big problem in factories in many developing nations. The International Labour Organization agreed to monitor them and to help companies meet the standards and correct the problems. As a result of the agreement, working conditions vastly improved; employment skyrocketed, producing new jobs for 270,000 workers (two-thirds of the industrial workforce); and exports to the United States increased 17 percent, through participating companies like Gap Inc., Nike, Sears, and others.

In 2005, the global system that established nation-by-nation quotas for access to U.S. and other wealthy markets expired, raising fears that Cambodia would lose its market share in the United States to lower-cost producers, mostly in China. Cambodia chose not to abandon its commitment to the high standards when the quotas expired, instead emphasizing the "brand security" that fair working conditions offer to buyers and trying to improve productivity. Apparently the companies agree, believing that it is both morally right to maintain the high standards, and a marketing asset to discerning U.S. and European consumers.

Before the quotas expired, Cambodia and the companies buying its clothing got some support for continuing this course from Global Fairness Initiative. Global Fairness is committed to making the global economy work for all through raising living standards in poor nations and maintaining a healthy middle class in wealthier ones. It brought together executives from garment companies, and government and multilaterals like the World Bank with trade experts in Cambodia to highlight Cambodia's labor practices as a model for development and an asset for business. The International Labour Organization is helping to extend the Cambodia model to Morocco, Romania, and the Philippines. Madagascar has started a similar program, and Global Fairness is working to establish similar standards in Central America. All this would not be possible without the willingness of U.S. clothing companies to buy slightly more costly products in the belief that their customers will agree to pay a little more to ensure a decent workplace and standard of living in countries struggling to grow. When American consumers buy clothing made in Cambodia, they know they're making the world a little more just.

Individuals can do this kind of work too. More than thirty-five years ago, the Cottrells, a young New Zealand couple, set up their own fair trade operation to create income for Tibetan refugee carpet makers in northern India by selling their work in New Zealand. Their NGO, Trade Aid, now runs a nationwide network of stores selling a variety of fair trade products, including hats and shawls from Bolivia, baskets from Uganda, and sculpture from Zimbabwe.

It's hard to describe any cell-phone market as organized, but its expansion into poor countries has had a very positive impact on local economies. A 2005 study found that every 10 percent increase in cell-phone penetration in a developing country increases per capita GDP by six-tenths of a percent, largely because people use it to get information that allows them to earn more money. Sudanese-born entrepreneur Mo Ibrahim made a fortune betting on the potential of cell phones in Africa. By 2005, 11 percent of the continent's population had access to them, with the number rising fast. Irish businessman Denis O'Brien is the largest cell-phone operator in Haiti. Young people now work selling time cards on the street, creating a whole new kind of employment for people desperate for jobs. The Grameen Bank has turned cell phones into a small-business opportunity by financing the purchase of at least one phone per village to a woman who then earns money by selling phone time to her neighbors.

In the United States, next to clean energy, the most underorganized and undercapitalized markets are those that employ and serve low-income people and neighborhoods in rural and urban areas. When I signed the Welfare Reform Act in 1996, requiring able-bodied people who could work to do so, there was legitimate concern that there would not be jobs available for them because they tended to be under-educated and to have less experience than most workers, and that when the economy slowed down, as it inevitably would, they would be the first laid off. While there have been some problems with the five-year lifetime benefit limit, and some people have dropped off both the welfare and employment rolls, welfare reform has been largely successful. The welfare rolls had dropped nearly 60 percent, more than seven million people, by the time I left office and have continued to drop since. The poverty rate among single mothers and the out-of-wedlock birthrate also declined, and the child poverty rate was the lowest since 1978. In 2000, the percentage of Americans on welfare reached its lowest point in four decades. During the economic downturn of 2001, many of those who came off the welfare rolls were able to stay in the workforce in part due to policies designed to help them succeed, including a doubling of the refundable earned income tax credit; a new child tax credit; an increase in the minimum wage; a doubling of child-support collections; a welfare-to-work tax credit to encourage employers to hire; more funds for child care, education, and training; the removal of the employment disincentives from Medicaid; transportation aid; and housing vouchers to help low-income people move closer to job opportunities. During my two terms, nearly 8 million people moved out of poverty, and the bottom 20 percent of earners saw their wages rise by 24 percent after falling 10 percent in the previous twelve years.

The success of welfare reform was due to more than better policies. There was also a conscious effort to expand the job market for people coming off welfare by organizing a large number of employers to recruit and hire their new employees from the welfare ranks. The partnership was established by my friend Eli Segal, who had earlier set up the

AmeriCorps program. The Welfare to Work Partnership began in 1997 with several hundred businesses committed to hiring people off the welfare rolls. Thanks to Eli and the evangelical zeal of the partnership's charismatic president and CEO, Rodney Carroll, an African-American businessman who took a leave from his job at UPS, its membership increased to more than twenty thousand firms of all sizes. By the end of 2000, they had hired more than one million people from the public assistance rolls, UPS alone accounting for almost 66,000 of them. Even those numbers underestimate the impact of the partnership's effort. The publicity the partnership received and the good results the firms achieved doubtless encouraged other businesses to follow suit.

One of the employers, infoUSA of Omaha, Nebraska, a mass-mailing operation, has made a concerted effort to hire people who were on welfare, as well as people who are disabled or who have to support themselves after getting out of unsafe domestic situations. Since 2001, it has hired more than one thousand of them, many of whom have become long-term employees. InfoUSA works with the Iowa School for the Deaf to train hearing-impaired employees and helps get transportation assistance for those without cars. Transportation is free for the first thirty days, then costs $20 a month. The company also works with lending institutions to help employees buy their own cars, and with the state of Nebraska to make sure they get the child-care assistance for which they are qualified. InfoUSA provides counseling and advice on how to get protective orders for employees who are victims of abuse. A couple of years ago I had the chance to visit with infoUSA's employees, and they seemed happy and self-confident, clearly enjoying their work. The Welfare to Work Partnership organized and expanded the job market for people who desperately wanted to escape welfare and build independent lives.

As president, I worked to bring distressed communities as well as welfare recipients into the economic mainstream with incentives like the Empowerment Zone and New Markets tax credits, and the establishment of community development banks, and microenterprise lending programs. After I left office, my foundation continued this work through the Urban Enterprise Initiative outlined in chapter 8, helping low-income workers qualify for the earned income tax credit and trying to move them away from dealing with excessively expensive lending and check-cashing operations and into becoming part of the financial mainstream.

While government incentives and foundation efforts in these areas are helpful, the truth is there is money to be made by investing in underserved communities and groups. Since leaving pro basketball, Magic Johnson has done very well investing in minority communities, including Harlem. So has Ron Burkle, founder of Yucaipa investment fund, which has earned strong returns for its labor union and public pension funds investors by targeting underserved communities and troubled companies with worker-friendly policies. When I left office, the opportunity to work with Yucaipa was the only private sector offer I accepted, because I wanted to continue working to bring economic opportunities to low-income communities, and I thought Yucaipa could prove they're good investments. In the last five years, Yucaipa brought Piccadilly Cafeterias, a largely Southern cafeteria chain, out of bankruptcy, saving almost six thousand jobs and creating more than five hundred new ones in fifteen states. Seventy-four percent of its communities are lower-income and underserved. Sixty-five percent of its employees, including 55 percent of those in management, are minorities. Yucaipa also bought Pathmark Supermarkets, which employs 26,000 people, half of them in underserved communities. Because of its purchase, Yucaipa may have saved many jobs because it did not sell off Pathmark's assets, which would have displaced thousands of employees.

On April 26, 2007, the *New York Times* carried a story on the efforts of Amalgamated Bank to open branch banks in neighborhoods with many people who have never had a bank account. There are an estimated 28 million of them in the United States, keeping their extra money at home, cashing their paychecks at costly check-cashing businesses, never having a checking or savings account or an ATM card. Often they borrow against coming tax refunds or paychecks— refund anticipation and pay-stub loans—which can lead to fees and interest rates totaling 40 to 400 percent. People who live in an all-cash economy are not just at greater risk of financial ruin; they can't establish a good credit rating or buy homes. The early returns on Amalgamated's outreach to the underserved is encouraging. Its new customers like earning interest on their money and paying lower rates when they borrow. The bank's president, Derrick Cephas, says he expects to turn a profit within a year. The article cited several examples of the benefits to first-time bankers. Jacqueline Williams, a telephone company employee, is relieved not to have to keep paying "thousands and thousands" of dollars to check-cashing businesses or to remember every place she stashed her money. Her ten-year-old son is excited that the $130 he saved will now earn interest. Sylvia Williams has used a check-cashing operation for twenty-seven years. She's happy to have her first ATM card at much less cost. There are millions of people like Sylvia and Jacqueline all over America who work hard, save money, and still remain unbanked. It's a market waiting to be developed, and its success will benefit all of us. This is a project ready-made for community organizations, religious congregations, and innovative, socially responsible businesses.

ELEVEN

Nonprofit Markets Can Be Organized Too

———————

THE SAME STRATEGIES businesses use to organize and expand markets that enhance the public good and empower their customers to do the same can be adopted by nongovernmental organizations involved in philanthropic work. By doing so, NGOs can help a lot more people and dramatically increase the impact of their donors' time and money. I hope that describing some of my foundation's efforts to organize markets will help you think of this as a new and different way of giving, and encourage you to support or start your own similar efforts, which may not require massive sums of money or time but can make a dramatic impact.

When I set up my foundation, I didn't know that many of the good things we would accomplish in the last six years would result from the application of such strategies to everything from AIDS drugs, tests, and testing equipment; to Rwandan farmers' fertilizer costs and microcredit interest rates; to the kinds of drinks and snacks available in American schools; and this year, I hope, to clean energy products on every continent.

After Nelson Mandela and I closed the World AIDS Conference in Barcelona in 2002, Prime Minister Denzil Douglas of St. Kitts and Nevis asked me to help the Caribbean nations establish and fund systems for the prevention, care, and treatment of HIV/AIDS. I agreed to do what I could, but with limited staffing in Harlem and Little Rock and an already crowded list of commitments, I needed some help. I called my friend Ira Magaziner, who had spearheaded our efforts in health care and e-commerce in the White House, and asked him to organize and lead the project.

I had known Ira since the late 1960s, when we were students at Oxford. From 1979 until he came to work in the White House, he founded and ran two successful corporate strategy firms with clients all across the world and wrote three books about the challenges of the emerging global economy. His long years of experience in the business world, his work on health care and electronic commerce in the White House, and his amazing ability to analyze complex problems and come up with creative solutions made him the perfect person for the job. I was especially glad Ira was able to take on this challenge because I always thought he took an unfair share of the blame for the defeat of my health-care plan in 1994. As I explained in my memoir, our effort to reduce costs and cover everyone was killed by politics, not by the plan's particulars. Since 2000, all the cost and coverage problems have worsened, and there is a growing consensus among business, labor, consumers, and health-care providers that we finally have to change our system to rein in costs, cover everyone, and promote wellness, in addition to treating sickness. I am optimistic that we will finally address the challenge in the next couple of years. Meanwhile, Ira Magaziner is busy saving the lives of people with AIDS.

Initially, the plan we developed called for assembling volunteers to work with governments that asked for our help to increase care and treatment, beginning in the Caribbean. As we were getting organized, I asked wealthier nations to commit the funds necessary to upgrade and expand developing nations' health services and to fund the purchase of generic drugs. Ireland and Canada were our first donors, followed by Norway, Sweden, and France, with other nations contributing lesser amounts. The foundation's expenses were covered by private citizens' donations from the United States, Canada, the United Kingdom, Ireland, and other nations.

We decided to buy generic antiretroviral medicines because they were so much less expensive, about $300 per person per year at the time. The government of the Bahamas was already providing generics to a few hundred people. Unbelievably, they were paying $3,500 per person per year for the $300 medicine because it was passing through two middlemen who were taking huge markups, showing just how disorganized the market was. We fixed that right away, enabling the Bahamas to buy almost ten times as many ARV pills with the same amount of money.

Then Ira set out to organize and enlarge the market. Enlisting the help of retired manufacturing executives, he worked with the major generic producers in India and South Africa to improve productivity and the efficiency of the supply chain and to negotiate a price reduction from $300 to $139. The manufacturers and suppliers of essential ingredients—Cipla, Ranbaxy, Aspen PharmaCare, Hetero, and Matrix—agreed to shift from a low-volume, high-margin, uncertain-payment business to a high-volume, low-margin, certain-payment one. Soon Ira and his team had also negotiated an 80 percent reduction in the cost of diagnostic testing and equipment with the major U.S. and European suppliers. Later negotiations led to reductions in the cost of the rapid HIV test from about $1 to between 49 and 65 cents; in some second-line drugs that have to be taken when the initial medications are no longer effective; and in pediatric AIDS medicine, from $600 to $196. In 2006, France imposed a small airline tax to raise funds to improve global health. Several other nations pledged contributions to the new program, known as UNITAID. The French asked our foundation to lead the UNITAID pediatric AIDS effort and committed $35 million to pay for the medicine. With the prospect of a huge expansion in the market, another round of negotiations cut the price of certain children's medicine to $60 per child per year, just 10 percent of what it had been two years earlier.

Today our foundation's AIDS initiative has more than six hundred people supporting its work in twenty-five nations. The rapid growth has required a great deal of help from donors. Canadian businessman Frank Giustra has given and raised millions to support this lifesaving work, and Chicago media executive Fred Eychaner singlehandedly funded all our operations in China for three years. Ukrainian businessman Victor Pinchuk and his wife, Elena Franchuk, fund all our operations there. Many others, including groups of Irish, Spanish, and Mexican businesspeople, have given generously. In 2004, we broadened access to our prices to other nations that committed to follow the international quality standards for care established by our Procurement Consortium agreement. So far sixty-nine countries have joined, and are now able to treat two to three times as many people with the same amount of money.

As I write this, almost 750,000 people are receiving treatment with drugs purchased under our contract terms, about a third of all those receiving treatment in the developing world today. The lower price our partners set and the big sales increases they sparked had a ripple effect on the market, accelerating considerable price decreases for other purchasers of AIDS generics. Now the average price listed by suppliers for the most common medicine is within our ceiling, so that even nations not part of our buying group can treat many more people within their budgets.

With the average price of the most common combination of adult drugs now down to about $120 a year and the price of children's medication down to $60, there are sufficient funds available for the drugs to treat most people in poor countries. We haven't yet negotiated enough price reductions for the second-line drugs, which cost on average more than ten times as much as the first-line medicines. By 2010, 10 percent of those on ARVs will be on second-line drugs. Beyond that, the main constraint on providing treatment is the limited ability of developing nations' health systems to identify and care for HIV-positive people. That's why we need more volunteers and donations.

Bolstered by our experience with AIDS drugs, our foundation and partners have used the strategy of organizing and expanding markets to advance other good causes. That's what we did for Rwandan farmers in the Clinton-Hunter Development Initiative in cutting the cost of fertilizer supplied by a Norwegian manufacturer 30 percent, reducing microcredit loan interest rates 30 to 50 percent, bringing greater efficiencies to the supply chain, and lowering transportation costs. As a result, Rwandan farmers had access to three and a half times more fertilizer than ever before at dramatically lower prices, despite the general trend of rising prices for both energy and fertilizer.

The public goods market was reorganized in a different way when the major soft drink and snack companies agreed with our foundation's Alliance for a Healthier Generation voluntarily to limit the caloric and sugar content of the products they sell in schools by reducing the size and improving the content of their products. Because major food producers including Campbell Soup, Dannon, Kraft Foods, Mars, and PepsiCo agreed to follow the same nutrition guidelines, and the American Beverage Association, PepsiCo, Coca-Cola, and Cadbury Schweppes all committed to follow the healthier school beverage guidelines, they will be able to help turn the tide of childhood obesity without being at a competitive disadvantage.

In 2006, Ken Livingstone, the mayor of London, asked our foundation to become involved with an effort he was organizing to get the world's largest cities to work together to combat climate change by becoming more energy-efficient and using more clean energy. To date, forty cities across the world are participating, along with more than a dozen smaller associate cities. In May 2007, we announced an effort to dramatically accelerate the greening of existing buildings. Beginning in sixteen of the forty cities, with five banks committing $1 billion each to finance the operations, the effort will more than double the current rate of building retrofitting. We also hope to help cities purchase LED traffic lights or high-pressure sodium street lights, and, in cities in developing nations, fund more efficient water systems and use methane from garbage dumps as a power source to generate electricity. Will it work? I hope so.

Individuals with ideas and skills but without a lot of money can also organize public goods markets. After my 2006 Global Initiative, Amos Olagunju wrote me to say he would use his professional training to build water supplies and help extend power to poor villages in his native Nigeria. Sergey Zhabin wrote to say he intended to link U.S. hospitals to specific hospitals in Africa to provide mentoring, sur-

plus supplies, and equipment. A woman who identified herself only as Mary said she would organize her community to
set up Parent Stress Lines, staffed by trained volunteers, to
help families having a hard time coping with loss, separation,
poverty, and abuse. In different ways, all these people are
increasing the public good by bringing order to an area of
need where it did not exist before.

The gift of a larger, better-organized public goods market, more accessible to consumers, whether given by a business leader like Lee Scott or Jeff Immelt, innovative labor
unions and public pension fund investors, an advocate like
Amory Lovins, a worker-friendly NGO like Global Fairness, or a brilliant social entrepreneur like Ira Magaziner,
can do a world of good. In doing so, they give everyone else
the opportunity to participate, by changing the way you consume energy and buy products, or by giving you the chance
to increase the impact of a donation of time, skills, or money.

TWELVE

What About Government?

———

N O BOOK ABOUT public service by private citizens would be complete without recognizing the
essential role of government—its laws, regulations, programs, and grants—in advancing the common
good and the importance of citizen activism in securing
good government. Good economic policies can enhance
business and job creation, decrease inequality of incomes,
ensure the benefits of free and fair trade, and accelerate the
development of new technologies. Social Security checks are
the difference between living above or below the poverty
line for almost half of America's senior citizens. Medicare
and Medicaid cover the health-care costs of tens of millions
of Americans who otherwise could not afford them. Almost
60 percent of the new drugs in the last decade were developed through government-funded research at our national
laboratories or universities. The quality of the air we
breathe, the food we eat, the water we drink is far better than
it would be without government regulations. Without government oversight, our workplaces would be less safe, our

185

stock and commodities markets less honest and transparent, and our travel more hazardous. We depend on government to finance the education of more than 90 percent of our children through high school and the higher education offered at public colleges and universities. We need government to maintain our national parks and protect priceless natural treasures; to keep our streets safe; to guarantee the civil rights of racial minorities, the disabled, and others; and, of course, to maintain our national security by protecting us from enemies and making a world with more partners and fewer enemies.

Just during my eight years as president, 35 million Americans used the Family and Medical Leave Act when a baby was born or a family member was sick; 43 million more citizens breathed air that met federal standards; 40 million more had access to safer drinking water; 85 million Americans in federally funded health plans got the protection of the Patients' Bill of Rights; 10 million more students received college aid; more than 2 million children were lifted out of poverty through the doubling of the earned income tax credit; for the first time, 90 percent of young children were immunized against serious diseases; 58 million acres of our national forests were protected under the Roadless Rule; and more than 1 million felons, fugitives, and stalkers were denied the ability to buy a handgun under the Brady Law.

Government matters. When it works well, citizen service can reinforce and supplement its efforts. When it doesn't work well, citizen service has a tougher hill to climb, in order to fill in the gaps in the social fabric. That's why one of the most important ways of giving time, money, knowledge, and skills can be in an effort to change, improve, or protect a government policy.

America has five big challenges that require an aggressive

response from government: 1) how to work with others to fight terror, the spread of weapons of mass destruction, and the consequences of failed or lawless states not just by opposing them militarily but also with diplomacy, aid, trade, and investment to build a world with more partners and fewer enemies; 2) how to restore our leadership in the global fight against climate change so that we do all we can and encourage China, India, and other populous developing nations with rising energy use to join us; 3) how to increase economic opportunity and decrease income inequality at home; 4) how to reform health care to achieve universal coverage that can't be taken away, with enough cost reductions to remain competitive, and a renewed emphasis on keeping people healthy, not just treating them when they are ill; and 5) how to move to a clean, more independent energy future in a way that increases our national security, combats climate change, and creates millions of new jobs.

Bono became a well-known figure in the United States, even among those unfamiliar with U2's music, by becoming an advocate in the first challenge, building a world in which more people are empowered to live positive, productive lives that are less vulnerable to siren calls to terror and violence. In 2000, he spent many hours talking to members of both parties in Congress on behalf of the millennium debt relief initiative to forgive the debts of the world's poorest countries if they observed basic human rights and put the savings into health, education, and economic development. One of the rock star's converts was Senator Jesse Helms, the very conservative chairman of the Foreign Relations Committee. When President George W. Bush took office, Bono worked with the White House to make good on the president's commitment to spend $15 billion over five years fighting AIDS and lobbied Congress for its passage. In 2005, in the months before the G8 meeting in Scotland, Bono supported Prime Minister Blair's call for another round of debt relief for the poorest countries and a doubling of aid to Africa to $50 billion a year.

He has also found a way for you to participate. It's called the ONE Campaign. Its goal is to persuade the U.S. government to dedicate one percent of our national income to eliminating extreme poverty in developing nations. The campaign is trying to get as many Americans as possible to sign the ONE Declaration—so far, more than two million people have signed. To raise the visibility of global poverty as a voting issue for Americans as we move toward the 2008 election, Bono wants to increase the number to as high a level as possible. You could be one of the signers.

Another important anti-poverty advocacy group is Bread for the World, a bipartisan faith-based group with 58,000 members, including three thousand churches. Bread for the World writes nearly 250,000 letters to Congress every year on behalf of initiatives to reduce poverty, hunger, and AIDS in the world's poorest countries. For the last two years, it has supported President Bush's proposal to change the way American food aid is delivered. Current law requires all aid to be in food grown in the United States, with three-fourths of it to be shipped on U.S. flag vessels. Rising energy costs, complicated logistics, and administrative costs now consume more than 60 percent of our main food aid program. As a result, U.S. aid is feeding about 70 million people a year as compared with more than 90 million five years ago. Canada and Europe have been moving away from shipping their own food to Africa and Asia in favor of giving cash to buy food in developing countries closest to places with severe hunger problems. That buys more food, gets it delivered more quickly, and helps poor farm economies. Canada is now providing half its food aid in this way, with the support of its major farm organizations. President Bush has proposed doing the same thing with 25 percent of U.S. food aid.

Unfortunately, farm groups and even some charities opposed the idea at first and for two years it's gone nowhere in Congress. Bread for the World hasn't given up. It has already converted some of its opponents and will keep trying. I have always supported farm programs that enable us to compete with heavily subsidized farms from Europe, Canada, and elsewhere. And I support the American maritime industry. But in this case, with a small change in the law and minimal loss to American farmers and shippers, we can provide food to save more lives—perhaps as many as fifty thousand a year—and help farmers in poor countries feed their neighbors. If you agree, you should contact Bread for the World and offer to help.

Al Gore has been working for changes in policy on climate change for twenty years or more, in and out of government. His film, *An Inconvenient Truth*, makes it clear that we need *both* citizen action and better policies. A number of business leaders, including several utilities with coal-fired plants, have joined in the call for the United States to set limits on carbon emissions and set up a system to trade emissions credits so that firms who can cut their emissions more easily can sell their emissions reductions above the cap to those who are having more trouble making it. Ceres, a network of investors, environmental organizations, and public interest groups, is also calling on Congress to act. Large institutional investors—Wall Street firms, insurance and reinsurance companies, and big state employee retirement systems—are ready to invest in clean energy but they have a fiduciary responsibility to their clients that requires them to know what long-term government policy will be. Progressive church leaders have for years supported a more vigorous response to climate change. Now a good number of evangelicals are joining in. Last year more than thirty of them signed an ad in the *New York Times* calling for action. Major environmental groups like the Natural Resources Defense Council, the Sierra Club, Environmental Defense, Greenpeace, and others have been supporting a more aggressive approach for a long time. The new Congress is beginning to act. For example, it is working with environmentalists and manufacturers on a new lighting standard that would phase out common incandescent lightbulbs over the next ten years, a change that would bring major reductions in electric bills and greenhouse gas emissions. The reductions in electricity demand will be enormous, the equivalent of the power now supplied by eighty coal-fired generators! If you want to help in lobbying the White House or Congress, you can get involved through any of the organizations mentioned in this paragraph.

In early 2007, an unusual coalition of business and labor leaders called Better Health Care Together held a press conference in which they announced a set of principles supporting health-care reform, including universal coverage and measures to rein in excessive costs. The group included Wal-Mart, AT&T, Intel, Kelly Services, the Communications Workers of America union, the Service Employees International Union, the Howard H. Baker, Jr., Center for Public Policy, and the Center for American Progress, run by my former chief of staff John Podesta. Even some of the health insurance companies have expressed a willingness to be part of the solution. The combined impact of premiums rising almost 90 percent since 2000, the increase in working families without insurance and millions more underinsured, and the threat to our economy, especially to manufacturing, of spending 50 percent more on health care than any other nation and getting less for it, may have finally given us the opportunity to build the health-care system Americans need and deserve. But it won't be easy. The devil will be in the details, especially in how to cut administrative costs that no other nation tolerates and in how to restrain prices far higher than even the wealthiest other nations pay. If you want to get involved in the fight for health-care reform, you can join the AARP if you're fifty or older and participate in its lobbying efforts, or contact Families USA, whose leader, Ron Pollack, has been agitating for reform for many years.

There are also many good groups that work for more specific changes in health policy. One of the most effective is the National Breast Cancer Coalition, founded in 1991 by a group of dedicated women, one of whom, Fran Visco, a breast cancer survivor, is its president. Visco has become a world-class advocate. Since its inception, the NBCC has created a nationwide grassroots advocacy network of more than six hundred organizations and seventy thousand breast cancer activists who lobby at the national, state, and local levels for public policies that improve breast cancer research, diagnostics, and treatment. Federal funding for breast cancer research increased from less than $90 million in 1991 to more than $800 million in 2003. When it was revealed that women in the military were more likely to develop breast cancer, NBCC lobbied for a special research project within the Department of Defense that secured about $2 billion in total funding. In 1993, the organization also produced and presented to me 2.6 million signatures supporting a National Action Plan on Breast Cancer involving government, private industry, scientists, and consumers. I accepted their proposal. In 2003, NBCC was the only grassroots organization cited as one of the twenty-five most influential groups in health policy in a survey of congressional staffers.

In 1996, Beth Kobliner Shaw, a New Yorker who has

written a highly regarded book on saving and investing for young people in the workplace, learned that her father had prostate cancer. Besides becoming actively involved in her father's care and treatment, she immersed herself in the state of prostate cancer research. When she discovered that despite the high prevalence of prostate cancer in men, there was wide disparity in federal funding for prostate cancer as opposed to breast cancer, she joined the National Prostate Cancer Coalition and became a one-woman campaign to convince the White House, and me personally, to close the gap. The Prostate Cancer Foundation credited her efforts for helping to gain a twenty-five-fold increase in government funding. Both Fran Visco and Beth Kobliner Shaw were private citizens living their own lives until cancer struck. Their response to it was to become highly committed and effective public servants. They prove just how much you can do if you have a cause you care about as much as they care about theirs.

Many working parents are having a hard time today. After staying essentially flat between 1979 and 1993, real family income rose each of the last seven years of the decade—over $8,000 per family—though it has fallen again by $1,300 since 2000, while much of our increased consumption has been fueled by maxed-out credit cards and second mortgages on homes. There were 5.37 million people who fell into poverty from 2000 to 2005; during the same time, there were 6.8 million more people without health insurance. More than half the bankruptcies of the last few years were caused by health emergencies. And the average wage of new jobs created in this decade is more than 20 percent below the average wage of jobs lost.

All these developments occurred when the economy was growing, worker productivity was increasing, and corporate profits reached a forty-year high. Part of the problem is that we haven't created enough good new jobs in the decade, largely because we haven't made an all-out commitment to a clean, efficient, independent energy future. The rest of the problem is rooted in changes in government policy and corporate conduct. We have finally raised the minimum wage for the first time in a decade, but we no longer have a manufacturing strategy, don't enforce our trade laws as vigorously, and don't provide adequate support and retraining to displaced workers. Unlike previous recoveries, this time working families are not gaining ground. The share of national income going to workers is the lowest on record, while the share of national income going to corporate profits is the highest on record. The Center on Budget and Policy Priorities reported that as of 2006, wages and salaries paid to workers as a percentage of GDP stands at the lowest level on record, 51.6 percent. The share of income going to corporate profits was the highest on record at 13.8 percent. In fact, slow wage growth is boosting corporate profits. According to Goldman Sachs, slow growth in labor compensation explains 64 percent of the increase in profit margins over the past year, and "the most important contributor to higher profit margins over the past five years has been a decline in labor's share of national income."

If you're interested in policy changes that would strengthen the middle class and help poor people work their way into it, you can contact the Center for American Progress, which is working on ways to lift the debt burdens on the middle class; the Center for Responsible Lending; ACORN, which organizes low-income people for economic and political empowerment; and several progressive religious groups, including the National Council of Churches, Catholics in Alliance for the Common Good, Faith in Public Life, and Sojourners.

America has hundreds of such advocacy groups that argue for better care for veterans of Iraq and Afghanistan; better equipment for our soldiers in combat; a stronger effort for peace in the Middle East; more rights for people with disabilities, as well as for gays, lesbians, and others; a fair and more effective immigration policy; greater education opportunities for minorities and the poor; and any number of other causes. Whether you're a Democrat, a Republican, or an Independent, a liberal, a conservative, or a moderate, you ought to find some positive change in government you can support. Groups that advocate for your views are not hard to find on the Internet, especially with all the aggressive blog sites exploding in cyberspace.

It's important to remember that some of your most significant advocacy and involvement can be at the state and local levels. The major health-care reforms of the last few years have been instituted by state governments, with several states poised to do more this year if the child-health insurance program's federal matching funds are continued. Groups of states in the West and the Northeast are trying to work together on climate change.

In April 2007, New York governor Eliot Spitzer proposed a package of legislative and regulatory measures designed to reduce the state's energy consumption below current levels by 2015, primarily through more renewable energy production and higher standards for appliances and buildings. A New York company, Empire State Wind Energy, founded by businessman Tom Golisano, is offering local governments the chance to own their own wind generators, sell the power to utilities, and use the earnings to reduce property taxes or finance public improvements.

In 2006, the California legislature under the leadership of Speaker Fabian Núñez and Senate President Pro Tempore Don Perata passed the most far-reaching climate change legislation in America. Around the same time, a citizen coalition of consumer, environmental, and public health groups, scientists, and business groups tried to accelerate the transformation with Proposition 87, a ballot initiative that would have imposed an extraction tax of between 1.5 percent and 6 percent on oil producers in California to raise $4 billion for clean fuel vehicles and fuel distribution networks; more rapid development of solar, wind, and hydrogen power; and more research for the development of new clean energy technologies. The ballot initiative was funded by philanthropist Steve Bing, who put $50 million into the effort. Unfortunately, it was defeated by the oil companies, which spent more than $100 million to convince voters that the extraction tax would raise their fuel bills (it wouldn't; every other oil-producing state already has one, and oil prices are set in global markets). The efforts have inspired support from millions of Californians who wanted clean energy, clean air, and thousands of new jobs in new energy fields. They have continued to push for more rapid progress, and their efforts have not been in vain.

In every state there are local groups or state affiliates of national ones working for changes in health-care and energy policy. They're usually looking for all the support they can get.

On climate change, however, most of the action has been at the local level. After President Bush rejected the mandatory emissions limits of Kyoto, about five hundred cities with Democratic and Republican mayors, under the leadership of Seattle mayor Greg Nickels, signed on to the Mayors Climate Protection Agreement to meet the Kyoto targets in their communities.

For example, Los Angeles has a vigorous strategy to reduce emissions in a way that will create jobs, cut utility bills, and improve the city's air quality and quality of life.

Under the leadership of its impressive young mayor, Antonio Villaraigosa, the city intends to produce 20 percent of the electricity its municipally owned utility sells from renewable sources by 2010 and retrofit existing plants to reduce emissions; reduce air pollution at its port and airport through the use of alternative fuels, greater efficiency, and more use of electric equipment; plant a million trees and increase open green space; convert more city vehicles to alternative fuels, including, by 2010, all the trucks that collect trash; increase the number of green building and green roofs, which will both conserve energy and lower power bills; expand mass transit; consume less water and recycle more solid waste; and support education programs to teach public school students how to conserve, reuse, and recycle.

Led by Mayor Michael Coleman, Columbus, Ohio, has redeveloped a closed department store with more than one million square feet into one of the nation's largest LEED (Leadership in Energy and Environmental Design) registered green buildings to house educational, governmental, and commercial facilities. Chicago is planting a lot of trees and striving to green as many rooftops of old buildings as possible, dramatically reducing energy use, greenhouse gas emissions, and utility bills. New Orleans has asked our foundation's Climate Change Initiative to support its efforts to "build back better" with sustainable housing projects and schools, the development of green building rehabilitation plans, and a training program in green rebuilding with an emphasis on minority contractors.

Boulder, Colorado, voters approved the nation's first municipal energy tax, averaging $1.33 per month on home electricity bills and $3.80 per month on business bills, to raise $1 million a year until it expires in 2012 to fund the city's Climate Action Plan. Investments in efficiency, renewable energy, and alternative fuel vehicles will cut greenhouse gases and save an estimated $63 million in energy costs, a return of ten to one on the $6 million tax investment.

New York City's emissions are already less than one-third of the national average on a per capita basis. Nevertheless the city has reduced its emissions another 446,000 metric tons a year through the use of hybrid and clean fuel vehicles, more energy-efficient equipment, and planting street trees. In April 2007, Mayor Michael Bloomberg released a comprehensive blueprint to make New York "the first environmentally sustainable twenty-first-century city." Its most controversial provision calls for an $8 a day "congestion pricing" charge for people who drive into Manhattan below Eighty-sixth Street. Similar plans have reduced congestion, and emissions, in London and Singapore. The funds raised from the fee would finance major mass transit projects. Most of New York's remaining emissions, about 80 percent of the total, are generated by buildings, two and a half times the U.S. average of 32 percent. New York plans a vigorous effort to reduce the emissions by another 30 percent by decreasing energy use in its buildings through computer controls on heating, air-conditioning, and lighting; green roofing; and other conservation measures. The city has 950,000 buildings. A crash plan to upgrade them with green roofs and more efficient lighting and windows would create a huge number of jobs and lower electric bills substantially for businesses and consumers.

Michigan is determined to lead the United States into a new era of clean energy and economic opportunity through NextEnergy, a nonprofit corporation founded in 2002 to advance alternative energy technologies in the automotive, electric power, and defense industries. NextEnergy is located in downtown Detroit's TechTown, a village for high-tech entrepreneurs established (and now being expanded) by

Mayor Kwame Kilpatrick, Wayne State University, General Motors, and Henry Ford Health System. NextEnergy offers entrepreneurs access to federal and private funding, laboratories, and testing equipment, access to research partners, and support in marketing viable technologies. I toured NextEnergy in April 2007 and saw an amazing array of new products, from hydrogen vehicles developed by the Big Three automakers and independent entrepreneurs, to more efficient solar and wind technologies, to more transformers, and other commercial and consumer products.

In 2006, the National Geographic's *Green Guide* ranked the following cities as the top ten in providing energy-efficient, low-pollution, healthy living spaces: Eugene, Oregon; Austin, Texas; Portland, Oregon; St. Paul, Minnesota; Santa Rosa, California; Oakland, California; Berkeley, California; Honolulu, Hawaii; Huntsville, Alabama; and Denver, Colorado. Eugene ranked first because 85 percent of its electricity is generated from hydro and wind power, the city's vehicle fleets are bio-diesel and hybrid, and there is a great deal of green space. Of course, most cities don't have access to hydropower, but hundreds of them are in hot pursuit of a green future.

Cities all over the world are going green. As I said earlier, my foundation's Climate Change Initiative is working with forty of them to reduce greenhouse gas emissions, beginning with an ambitious building retrofit program backed by $5 billion in financing commitments from big banks. The leader of the international effort, London mayor Ken Livingstone, is determined to reduce emissions to 60 percent below 1990 levels by 2025. Based on the progress he's already made and his commitment of more than $150 million over the next three years, I wouldn't bet against him.

The greening of cities offers many opportunities for citizen involvement. If your city hasn't made a specific commitment to reduce emissions to or below the Kyoto targets, you should start by working with like-minded citizens to persuade its leaders to do so, emphasizing the large number of opportunities to save money, create jobs, and meet our climate change responsibilities. If your community already has a conservation and clean energy plan, you can help with the implementation and by convincing as many of your fellow citizens as possible to participate in the effort. *The Citizen-Powered Energy Handbook* by Greg Pahl has some good ideas on how to start. So does the British NGO Green Alliance. Its Energy Entrepreneurs Network lobbies government at all levels to embrace new ideas and integrate environmental considerations into all aspects of public policy.

The quality of government—its capacity to provide basic services, its level of competence, its responsiveness to its citizens' aspirations and complaints, its adherence to the rule of law and openness to growth and change—is critical to the ability of citizens in developing countries to improve their lives and to the success of NGO activities and foreign assistance programs. Therefore the efforts of citizen groups who work to improve governance in developing nations is incredibly important. The Women Waging Peace Network's mission is to connect women from conflict areas around the world and to help them influence public policy. It was launched in 1999 by Swanee Hunt, one of the founding members of Vital Voices and ambassador to Austria in my first term as president. During her tenure, she became involved with women working for peace across ethnic lines in Bosnia and wrote about it in her book, *This Was Not Our War: Bosnian Women Reclaiming the Peace*. The Women Waging Peace Network grew out of that experience.

The network is supporting women peacemakers in places

like Sudan, Sri Lanka, Colombia, Sierra Leone, Bosnia, and the Middle East. Hunt's contention is that, in many conflict states, "women's status as second-class citizens is a source of empowerment, making them adept at finding innovative ways to cope with problems." For example, the network is supporting Nanda Pok in Cambodia, a nation still not fully recovered from the Khmer Rouge ravages of the 1970s that claimed almost two million lives. Pok wants women to lead her country to a brighter, fairer future. She has trained more than five thousand women to run for public office, including 64 percent of those who were elected to local councils in 2002.

Mo Ibrahim, founder of Celtel International and one of Africa's most successful businessmen, established a foundation to promote good governance in Africa. In 2007, he will award the first Mo Ibrahim Prize for Achievement in African Leadership, to recognize African leaders who have improved the lives of their people and strengthened conditions for sustainable economic and social development, including honest government and the rule of law, the empowerment of civil society, and advancements in health, education, and human rights. The prize, to be given after the leader leaves office, is $5 million over ten years and $200,000 a year thereafter for life, with the possibility of an additional $200,000 a year that the leader can direct to good causes. Ibrahim has also developed, in cooperation with the Kennedy School of Government at Harvard, an Index of African Governance to rank sub-Saharan countries according to comparative, objective criteria. He hopes the index will lead to improvements in governance across the continent as well as open debates about how governance can best be assessed. I hope concerned citizens in other regions will consider adapting Ibrahim's prize and index to their areas.

One of the most highly charged and highly publicized

forms of this kind of activism involves citizens of one country lobbying for changes in policies by the government of another country. For example, the families of victims of the Pan Am 103 bombing, which killed 270 people in an explosion over Lockerbie, Scotland, in 1988, have proved to be tenaciously effective in forcing the U.S. government to keep the pressure on the government of Libya, the home of the perpetrators, until the suspects were handed over for trial and the indemnity claims are paid in full. Because Libya is eager to shed its reputation as a sponsor of terrorism and to be reconciled with the United States, the families' vigilance was clearly a contributing factor to Libya's decision, after 9/11, to work with the British and U.S. governments to disclose and dismantle its weapons of mass destruction program.

Perhaps the most important current example of this kind of citizen activism involves the ongoing humanitarian tragedy in Sudan, where militia groups' conflicts with the central government and its militia allies, the Janjaweed, have disrupted life in the vast Darfur region of western Sudan, spawning 2.5 million refugees and claiming between 200,000 and 400,000 lives from violence and starvation. Most of the killing has been carried out by the Janjaweed with the tacit and sometimes active support of the national government. The refugees are packed together in relatively isolated camps, protected only by a small force of fewer than eight thousand African Union troops, mostly from Nigeria and Rwanda. The force is too small for the job, lacks proper communications equipment, and operates under a U.N. mandate that unduly restricts its ability to prevent violence against the African Muslim refugees by the Arab militia groups. Until early 2007, the Sudanese government successfully resisted a larger U.N. force, including non-African militaries, thanks largely to the support China has given its position in the U.N. Security Council.

The Darfur tragedy has prompted an outpouring of support for the refugees all across America, especially among college students, schoolchildren, African-American church congregations, and much of the entertainment community. Actors Don Cheadle and George Clooney have been especially active, traveling not only to Darfur but also to Egypt and China to try to persuade the governments there to support a stronger U.N. mission.

In early 2007, Mia Farrow, in her role as U.N. Children's Fund Goodwill Ambassador, tried a different tack to persuade the Chinese to change their position. She began referring to the 2008 Olympics to be hosted by China in Beijing as the "Genocide Olympics." She also asked Steven Spielberg, who is helping to plan the opening ceremonies, to weigh in with the Chinese, which he did. Hosting the Olympics is very important to the Chinese, who see it as an irreplaceable opportunity to showcase their history, culture, and progress to the world. Tying China's defense of Sudan's indefensible position to its hosting of the Olympics could seriously undermine what China hopes to gain from the games. Shortly after Farrow launched her barbs, the Chinese urged Sudan to work with U.N. secretary general Ban Ki-moon and the Arab League, led by Saudi Arabia, who want Sudan to accept a joint African Union–U.N. force of police, peacekeepers, and attack helicopters. In April 2007, the Sudanese finally agreed to accept a few thousand U.N. troops but not the full force of seventeen thousand or the attack helicopters. It's not enough and the forces aren't on the ground yet. But it's a start, thanks in part to the efforts of citizen activists as well as those of concerned governments. I think we'll see more of this kind of advocacy in the years ahead, and given our global media culture in which abuses of human rights can't be hidden, I believe the advocates—if they're persistent, practical, and creative—will often prevail. Most of us aren't public figures like Mia Farrow, Don Cheadle, or George Clooney who can use their fame to do good, but each of us has the ability to do something.

One final note on governance. Citizen support is becoming increasingly important to the United Nations and its affiliated agencies. While contributions from member governments fund the basic operations of the United Nations; the World Bank; the International Monetary Fund; the World Health Organization; the Global Fund to Fight AIDS, Tuberculosis, and Malaria; and others, the United Nations has taken on so many humanitarian operations that it also needs private support to be truly effective. For example, fees on airline tickets in France and several other countries fund UNITAID's campaign against AIDS, TB, and malaria; the Gates Foundation's support of the GAVI Alliance helps to provide more vaccines and immunizations to poor children; private donations increased UNICEF's ability to provide schooling, clean water, and nutrition to kids after the tsunami; and Nike and Microsoft helped design ninemillion.org for the U.N. High Commissioner for Refugees, to give average citizens the chance to help fund the education of 9 million children in refugee camps.

In 1998, the United Nations set up its own foundation to accept private contributions in support of its various causes. Though the U.N. Foundation's first gift was Ted Turner's historic $1 billion contribution, it solicits contributions at all levels, and thousands of people have responded, knowing that the money will be invested well, much of it in partnerships with NGOs.

THIRTEEN

How Much Should You
Give and Why?

————

THE DECEMBER 17, 2006, *New York Times Magazine* featured a fascinating article by philosopher Peter Singer entitled "What Should a Billionaire Give—and What Should You?" Singer says Warren Buffett has given away more than twice as much in inflation-adjusted dollars as the legendary philanthropists of a century ago, John D. Rockefeller and Andrew Carnegie. Bill Gates has already given away well over a third of his fortune. Buffett intends to give away over 95 percent of his, saying he wants to leave his children "enough so they feel they could do anything but not so much they could do nothing." Zell Kravinsky of Jenkintown, Pennsylvania, gave almost all of the $45 million he made in real estate to health-related charities when he was in his mid-forties, keeping only his home and enough to meet his family's living expenses. Then, when he learned that thousands of people die from kidney failure every year while waiting for a kidney transplant, he donated one of his own kidneys to a stranger. Kravinsky believes all lives are of equal value. Since the chances of dying as a result

of kidney donation are about one in four thousand, his decision made perfect sense to him.

Singer explained how wealthy Americans alone could pay
our nation's fair share to meet the Millennium Development
Goals without going as far as Buffett or Kravinsky. The estimated cost of the effort was $121 billion in 2006, rising to
$189 billion in 2015 (it's actually less, given the funds already
being spent and those that are pledged). Singer believes the
United States should pay at least 36 percent of the bill
because that's the percentage of U.S. domestic product of
the wealthiest nations that make up the Organisation for
Economic Co-operation and Development (our share of
global GDP is about 27 percent).

Working from 2004 U.S. tax data, he says that if the
14,400 taxpayers in the top .01 percent give a third of their
income (averaging $12,775,000) to combat the world's most
severe problems, the total would be about $61 billion. If the
top 0.1 percent, 129,600 taxpayers, give away a quarter of
their income (averaging just over $2 million), the giving
would total close to $65 billion. If the top 0.5 percent,
575,900 taxpayers, give 20 percent of their income, total
giving would be $72 billion. There are 719,900 in the top
one percent. If they give 15 percent, it would raise $35 bil-
lion. If the rest of the top 10 percent, 13 million of them
(with an average income of $132,000), give 10 percent, it
would come to about $171 billion. That's a total of $404 billion just from the top 10 percent of Americans. Singer then
argues that this $404 billion should be matched by contribu-
tions from wealthy individuals in other countries and their
governments, bringing the total to $808 billion, more than
six times what it would take to meet the goals. Singer
believes we should raise these goals and do more faster.

While Singer's analysis shows how America could pay

more than its fair share of the Millennium Goals budget from private giving alone, I think it's unrealistic to expect this level of giving to global causes in the short run, for several reasons: some wealthy people don't believe the money will be spent wisely (although I hope I've persuaded you in the previous chapters that it can be); some people with high incomes but little accumulated wealth want to build an estate before they give a large portion of their money away; $132,000 a year goes a lot further in Little Rock than it does in New York City; and many wealthy people are already committed to giving money to other charitable causes in America. U.S. foundations gave away more than $40 billion in 2006 alone.

Let's look at a more modest scenario. If the top one percent simply give 5 percent of their income to meet the goals, the top .01 percent would give $9.2 billion; the top 0.1 percent, $13 billion; the top 0.5 percent, $18 billion; the top one percent, $12 billion. If the rest of the top 10 percent give one percent of their incomes to the cause, it would raise another $17.2 billion. The total would be nearly $70 billion, more than enough to meet 36 percent of the cost of the goals, with more than $20 billion left over to support our fellow citizens who are tackling big problems at home. Also, if giving by the wealthiest Americans even approached these levels, I'm convinced it would spark an enormous outpouring of contributions from Americans of more modest means. Even if each gift is relatively small, millions of contributions from the other 90 percent, aided by the Internet, could equal or surpass the total giving by wealthy Americans.

The example of how much money we could give also applies to gifts of time, skills, things, reconciliation, and new beginnings. If we just all gave according to our ability, the positive impact would be staggering. I hope this book has given you a better idea of the options available for effective giving. In America, many of us are besieged by more requests for help than we can grant. All of us have to decide among competing claims on our time and money. Do we concentrate our resources on one project or spread them around? That is a choice that only you can make. But first you have to decide whether, and how much, to give.

Why do some people give so much while others give the bare minimum or not at all? I've thought about this a lot, and it seems to me we all give for a combination of reasons, rooted in what we think about the world in which we live and what we think about ourselves. We give because we think it will help people today or give our children a better future; because we feel morally obligated to do so out of religious or ethical convictions; because someone we know and respect asked us; or because we find it more rewarding and more enjoyable than spending more money on material possessions or more time on recreation or work.

When people don't give, I think the reasons are simply the reverse. They don't believe what they could do would make a difference, either because their resources are limited or they're convinced efforts to change other people's lives and conditions are futile. They don't feel morally obligated to give. No one has ever asked them to do so. And they believe they'll enjoy life more if they keep their money and time for themselves and their families.

I've done my best in this book to demonstrate that all kinds of giving can make a profoundly positive difference, that everyone has something valuable to give, and that countless individuals and organizations are asking for help. Of course, people have to make their own decisions about what they feel morally compelled to do and what will make them happy.

All religious faiths speak to our shared obligations to help one another. In Jewish law and tradition, giving, *tzedakah*, is obligatory, up to at least 10 percent of income. The literal meaning of the Hebrew word *tzedakah* is "righteousness," but it also is used to refer to justice and to giving to those in need. The righteous individual must strive for social justice through giving. The wide range of Jewish organizations, including the American Jewish World Service, the United Jewish Appeal, the Anti-Defamation League, and MAZON, giving staggering sums to promote good causes in their home nation, in Israel, and in poor nations across the world, demonstrates the powerful hold of *tzedakah* on the hearts of believers.

Islam also has made charity, *zakat*, obligatory for all those who embrace the faith. Muslims believe that all human beings should be one another's well-wishers, that the wealthy have a sacred duty to help the poor, disabled, and others in need, and that other Muslims do too, after first meeting the needs of their own family.

Beyond the obligatory giving of *zakat*, 2.5 percent of income and a higher percentage on physical possessions from food to jewelry, Muslims of means are morally bound to give more when the common good cannot be met by the *zakat* giving alone. The word for voluntary giving is *sadaqah*, which like the Hebrew word *tzedakah* means righteousness (how often we forget all we have in common!). Muslims are expected to remove stumbling blocks that keep others from living a full life and to do so voluntarily without self-promotion or earthly reward. The activities of local groups in the United States like the Inner-City Muslim Action Network of Chicago and the rise of modern universities and medical research institutions in the Persian Gulf reflect this kind of giving.

How Much Should You Give and Why?

All Christians are taught to tithe 10 percent of our income to the church and to love our neighbors as ourselves. From an early age, we are reminded over and over again that "it is more blessed to give than to receive." More and more Christian churches in America are expanding their giving activities beyond their congregations to the larger community in ways I've mentioned earlier. More and more Christian leaders are embracing the fight against climate change as our obligation to honor the biblical injunction to preserve the earth and its fruits for future generations. The great biologist E. O. Wilson's latest book, *The Creation*, is written as a letter from a secular scientist to an evangelical minister outlining their shared obligation to save the planet and all its life-forms.

More and more Christian organizations are reaching out across the world to help people regardless of their faith. Christian charitable groups labored mightily after the tsunami to help Muslims in Indonesia and Buddhists and Hindu Tamils in Sri Lanka. World Vision has 23,000 staff members working in almost one hundred countries to combat famine and child exploitation, provide education for poor children including equal opportunities for girls, and promote economic development. In 2006 alone, World Vision and its more than four and half million American supporters made more than 440,000 microcredit loans and more than $200 million in food grants.

All other faiths, in one form or another, teach the moral imperative of giving. Buddhists believe donation to others is an essential step on the path to full enlightenment. They believe a selfish nature devoid of charity retards development and that giving should benefit people who need it regardless of who and where they are, in a spirit of benevolence known as *Dana Paramita*. They teach that practicing charity without expecting anything in return is essential to creating a mind free of jealousy or hatred, something we all need.

Believer or nonbeliever, we all live in an interdependent world in which our survival depends upon an understanding that our common humanity is more important than our interesting and inevitable differences and that everyone matters. In Africa, where the first humans stood up on the savannah 150,000 years ago, some tribes have a remarkable way of greeting each other. When one person says hello, the response is "I see you." Think how much better the world would be if we actually saw each other.

Will giving make you happier? You'll have to answer that for yourself. When I was in Africa with Bill and Melinda Gates, watching them talk to villagers whose lives they had improved, they seemed happy. When I saw young Brianne Schwantes risk more broken bones in her fragile body to help people in the Mississippi flood, she seemed happy. When I watched John Bryant light up the eyes of poor kids with talk of how they could have different lives, he seemed happy. When I met Oseola McCarty after she gave her life savings so that young people could have the education she never had, she seemed happy. When Carlos Slim looked at a crowd of ten thousand young people he'd sent to college, he seemed happy. When Barbra Streisand and Rupert Murdoch, two highly public figures who disagree on nearly everything politically, stood together to give the first contributions to my foundation's fight against climate change, they seemed happy. When Chris and Basil Stamos, Chris Hohn and Jamie Cooper-Hohn, Frank Giustra and Fred Eychaner, and all the others who fund my AIDS work look into the eyes of children who are alive because of them, they seem happy.

So much of modern culture is characterized by stories of self-indulgence and self-destruction. So much of modern politics is focused not on honest differences of policy but on personal attacks. So much of modern media is dominated by people who earn fortunes by demeaning others, defining them by their worst moments, exploiting their agonies. Who's happier? The uniters or the dividers? The builders or the breakers? The givers or the takers?

I think you know the answer. There's a whole world out there that needs you, down the street or across the ocean. Give.

ACKNOWLEDGMENTS

As in the writing of *My Life*, I am most indebted to Justin Cooper for helping me gather and organize materials, doing extra research, correcting errors, and working on the manuscript over and over as I wrote and rewrote it in my notebooks. In the last three weeks of writing, Caitlin Klevorick also did an excellent job helping Justin with fact-checking.

My indefatigable editor, Bob Gottlieb, was again invaluable in reminding me to emphasize the human side of service work, pushing me to include more examples of giving that everyone could identify with, and purging my prose of as much policy-wonk speak as he could without making it his book instead of mine.

I am also grateful to others at Knopf for helping me bring this book to life: to Sonny Mehta, chairman and editor in chief, for believing the subject was worth a book; to Tony Chirico, president, for his support; to managing editor Katherine Hourigan for reading the manuscript and suggesting the addition of a few remarkable projects created by citizens whose only wealth was in the power of their ideas and commitment; and to Andy Hughes, Maria Massey, Jessica Freeman-Slade, and the many others who did the proofreading and put the book together.

I want to thank all those who read all or part of the book and offered suggestions, beginning with Hillary, Chelsea, and my mother-in-law, Dorothy Rodham; my lawyer Bob Barnett; and Doug Band, Sandy Berger, Ron Burkle, Tommy Caplan, Oscar Flores, Frank Giustra, Rolando González-Bunster, Laura Graham, Bruce Lindsey, Cheryl Mills, Eric Nonacs, John Podesta, Trooper Sanders, Gene Sperling, and Mark Weiner.

I am indebted to the people who provided information on their activities and to those who talked to me about why they do their giving. Most of them are quoted in the book.

Writing a book takes a lot of time. While I was at it, the work of my foundation, presidential library and center, the school of public service, and the Clinton Global Initiative continued apace, thanks to the devoted efforts of all those who work in those areas. I am profoundly grateful to all of them and want to especially thank Laura Graham, my chief of staff and representative to the Bush-Clinton Katrina and tsunami funds; Trooper Sanders, my liaison to the Alliance for a Healthier Generation, the Urban Enterprise Initiative, and the economic empowerment initiatives mentioned in the book; and Eric Nonacs, my foreign policy aide and liaison to the HIV/AIDS Initiative, Clinton-Hunter Development Initiative, and the Clinton Global Initiative. They always go above and beyond the call of duty.

Finally, I want to thank those whose gifts of time and money have made my work possible. Like the other givers chronicled in this book, they are old, young, and in-between, with incomes large, small, and in-between. Their gifts range from volunteering full-time to a few hours a week, from donating several million dollars to a few dollars. Without them, I couldn't have made much of my own gifts, and I will be forever grateful. I can only hope that their giving has made them as happy as they deserve to be for all the good they have done.

RESOURCES

1: *Private Citizens/Public Good*

WEB SITES

Amnesty International
amnesty.org

Bill and Melinda Gates
Foundation
gatesfoundation.org

Bush-Clinton Katrina Fund
bushclintonkatrinafund.org

The Carter Center
cartercenter.org

The Clinton Global Initiative
clintonglobalinitiative.org

Clinton Foundation HIV/AIDS
Initiative
clintonfoundation.org

Doctors Without Borders
doctorswithoutborders.org

Grameen Bank
grameen-info.org

The Green Belt Movement
greenbeltmovement.org

Greenpeace
greenpeace.org

Habitat for Humanity
habitat.org

ONE Campaign
one.org

Opportunity International
opportunity.org

Opportunity International
Australia
opportunity.org.au

Oxfam
oxfamamerica.org

Red Cross
redcross.org

The Self Employed Women's
Association (India)
sewa.org

ShoreBank Corporation
shorebankcorp.com

United Nations
http://www.un.org

The United Way
national.unitedway.org

The William J. Clinton
Foundation
clintonfoundation.org

The World Wildlife Fund
worldwildlife.org

Resources

BOOKS

Dowla, Asif, and Dipal Barua. *The Poor Always Pay Back: The Grameen II Story*. Bloomfield, Conn.: Kumarian Press, 2006.

Fine, Allison H. *Momentum: Igniting Social Change in the Connected Age*. San Francisco: Jossey-Bass, 2006.

Maathai, Wangari. *Unbowed*. New York: Alfred A. Knopf, 2006.

Rischard, J. F. *High Noon: Twenty Global Problems, Twenty Years to Solve Them*. New York: Basic Books, 2002.

Tocqueville, Alexis de. *Democracy in America*. New York: Everyman's Library, 1994.

Yunus, Muhammad. *Banker to the Poor: Micro-Lending and the Battle Against World Poverty*. New York: PublicAffairs, 1999.

2: Giving Money

WEB SITES

ARK (Absolute Return for Kids)
arkonline.org

American Heart Association
americanheart.org

American Institute of Philanthropy
charitywatch.org

Animal Rescue New Orleans
animalrescueneworleans.com

Bill and Melinda Gates
   Foundation
gatesfoundation.org

By Kids for Kids
bkfk.com

CancerCare
cancercare.org

Challah for Hunger
challahforhunger.org

Charity Navigator
charitynavigator.org

Chess-in-the-Schools
chessintheschools.org

Children's Investment Fund
   Foundation
ciff.org

Clinton Foundation HIV/AIDS
   Initiative
clintonfoundation.org

The Enterprise Community
   Partners
enterprisecommunity.org

Fertile Hope
fertilehope.org

Friends Without a Border
fwab.org

Give
give.org

Guidestar
guidestar.org

Harlem Children's Zone
hcz.org

Kids to the Rescue
kidstotherescue.org

Kitchen Table Charities Trust
kitchentablecharities.org

Kiva
kiva.org

The Lance Armstrong Foundation
livestrong.org

The National Office of Native
   Cancer Survivorship
oncs.org

Oprah's Angel Network
oprahsangelnetwork.org

Oprah Winfrey Leadership
    Academy Foundation
oprahwinfreyleadershipacademy
    .o-philanthropy.org

Oseola McCarty Scholarship Fund
usm.edu/pr/oolamain.htm

Partners In Health
pih.org

The Robin Hood Foundation
robinhood.org

Seeds of Peace
seedsofpeace.org

Susan Thompson Buffett
    Foundation
buffettscholarships.org

BOOKS

Cullman, Lewis B. *Can't Take It
with You: The Art of Making and
Giving Money.* Hoboken, N.J.:
John Wiley & Sons, 2004.

Fleishman, Joel L. *The Foundation.*
New York: PublicAffairs, 2007.

Zeiler, Freddi. *A Kid's Guide to
Giving.* Norwalk, Conn.:
Innovative Kids, 2006.

3: Giving Time

WEB SITES

ACORN
acorn.org

Alliance for a Healthier
    Generation
healthiergeneration.org

American Heart Association
americanheart.org

AmeriCorps
americorps.org

AmeriKids
campamerikids.org

Big Brothers Big Sisters
bbbsa.org

Bush-Clinton Katrina Fund
bushclintonkatrinafund.org

City Year
cityyear.org

Covenant House
covenanthouse.org

Doctors Without Borders
doctorswithoutborders.org

do-it.org.uk
do-it.org.uk

The Global Fund to Fight AIDS,
    Tuberculosis, and Malaria
http://www.theglobalfund.org

Google.org
google.org

Habitat for Humanity
habitat.org

The Heart of America Foundation
heartofamerica.org

Henry Street Settlement
henrystreet.org

Inter-Religious Fellowship for the
    Homeless of Bergen County
irfhomeless.org

Let's Just Play—Go Healthy
    Challenge
nick.com/letsjustplay

Los Angeles Conservation Corps
lacorps.org

Resources

Make-A-Wish Foundation
wish.org

National Obesity Forum (UK)
nationalobesityforum.org.uk

Orfalea Family Foundation
orfaleafamilyfoundation.org

Partners In Health
pih.org

The Peace Corps
peacecorps.gov

Project H.O.M.E.
projecthome.org

Red Cross
redcross.org

The Road Home
road2la.org

Robert Wood Johnson Foundation
rwjf.org

The Solar Electric Light Fund
self.org

University of Arkansas, Clinton
    School of Public Service
clintonschool.uasys.edu

Volunteer Match
volunteermatch.org

Volunteer Reading Help
vrh.org.uk

Volunteering Australia
volunteeringaustralia.org

Volunteering England
volunteering.org.uk

Volunteering New Zealand
volunteeringnz.org.nz

VSO
vso.org.uk

Yum-o! Organization
yum-o.org

BOOKS

Farmer, Paul. *Infections and Inequalities*. Berkeley: University of California Press, 1999.

Farmer, Paul. *Pathologies of Power: Health, Human Rights, and the New War on the Poor*. Berkeley: University of California Press, 2004.

Kidder, Tracy. *Mountains Beyond Mountains*. New York: Random House, 2003.

Kielburger, Craig, and Marc Kielburger. *Me to We: Finding Meaning in a Material World*. New York: Fireside, 2006.

Marshall, Will, and Marc Porter Magee, eds. *The AmeriCorps Experiment and the Future of National Service*. Washington, D.C.: Progressive Policy Institute, 2005.

May, Elizabeth. *How to Save the World in Your Spare Time*. Toronto: Key Porter Books, 2007.

4: Giving Things

WEB SITES

America's Second Harvest
    (Backpack Club)
secondharvest.org

Career Gear
careergear.org

Doc to Dock
doctodock.com

Dress for Success
dressforsuccess.org

eBay Giving Works
givingworks.ebay.com

Resources

The First Tee
thefirsttee.org

Goodwill
goodwill.org

House Ear Institute
hei.org

Locks of Love
locksoflove.org

Musicares
grammy.com/musicares

Music Rising
musicrising.org

Organization of Rural Associations
    for Progress (ORAP)
synergos.org/voices/orap1.html

Points of Light Foundation
pointsoflight.org

The Prostate Cancer Foundation
prostatecancerfoundation.org

Red Cross
redcross.org

Room to Read
roomtoread.org

Salvation Army
salvationarmyusa.org

Samaritan's Purse
samaritanspurse.org

Save the Children
savethechildren.org

UNICEF
unicef.org

U.S.-Africa Children's Fellowship
childrensfellowship.org

VH1 Save the Music Foundation
vh1.com/partners/save_the_music/

World Bicycle Relief
worldbicyclerelief.org

World Vision International
worldvision.org

Salbi, Zainab. *Between Two Worlds:
    Escape from Tyranny: Growing
    Up in the Shadow of Saddam.*
    New York: Gotham, 2005.

Wood, John. *Leaving Microsoft
    to Change the World.* New York:
    Collins, 2006.

5: Giving Skills

WEB SITES

ACORN
acorn.org

The Algebra Project
algebra.org

America Learns
americalearns.net

America Reads
ed.gov/inits/americareads

Andre Agassi Charitable
    Foundation
agassifoundation.org

Andre Agassi College Preparatory
    Academy
agassiprep.org

Boys and Girls Club of America
bgca.org

Business for Diplomatic Action
businessfordiplomaticaction.org

Efficacy Institute
efficacy.org

The Frederick Douglass Academy
fda1.org

Girls Incorporated
girlsinc.org

Resources

Home Instruction for Parents of
  Preschool Youngsters (HIPPY)
hippyusa.org

Mayo Clinic
mayoclinic.com

National Academy Foundation
naf.org

National Head Start Association
http://www.nhsa.org

Operation Hope
operationhope.org

Parents as Teachers
parentsasteachers.org

Reading Recovery
readingrecovery.org

Room to Read
roomtoread.org

Tiger Woods Foundation
twfound.org

Tiger Woods Learning Center
twlc.org

U.S.-Africa Children's Fellowship
childrensfellowship.org

Women for Women International
womenforwomen.org

Young Arab Leaders
yaleaders.org

BOOKS

Clinton, Hillary Rodham. *It Takes
  a Village*. Simon & Schuster,
  1996.

6: Reconciliation/New Beginnings

WEB SITES

Alcoholics Anonymous
alcoholics-anonymous.org

Annie E. Casey Foundation
http://www.aecf.org

Bard Prison Project
http://www.bard.edu/bpi

Bush-Clinton Katrina Fund
bushclintonkatrinafund.org

Bush-Clinton Houston Tsunami
  Fund
state.gov/r/pa/ei/pix/b/sa/45733
  .htm

Ford Foundation
fordfound.org

George Bush Presidential Library
  Foundation
http://www.georgebushfoundation
  .org/bush/

Interfaith Youth Core
ifyc.org

Jordan River Foundation
www.jordanriver.jo

PeacePlayers International
playingforpeace.org

The Pentecostals of Alexandria
thepentecostals.org

Public/Private Ventures
ppv.org

Ready4Work
ready4work.com

Seeds of Peace
seedsofpeace.org

U.S. Dream Academy, Inc.
usdreamacademy.com

Vital Voices Democracy
  Initiative
vitalvoices.org

BOOKS

Bane, Mary Jo, Brent Coffin, and
  Richard Higgins, eds. *Taking
  Faith Seriously*. Cambridge,
  Mass.: Harvard University
  Press, 2005.

Resources

O'Donnell, Beth, text by
Kimberley Sevcik. *Angels in
Africa*. New York: Vendome
Press, 2006.

Patel, Eboo, and Patrice Brodeur,
eds. *Building the Interfaith
Youth Movement*. Lanham,
Md.: Rowman & Littlefield,
2006.

Sider, Ronald J. *Just Generosity:
A New Vision for Overcoming
Poverty in America*. Grand
Rapids, Mich.: Baker Books,
1999.

Wallach, John, with Michael
Wallach. *The Enemy Has a
Face: The Seeds of Peace
Experience*. Washington, D.C.:
United States Institute of
Peace Press, 2000.

7: Gifts That Keep on Giving

WEB SITES

The Bernard and Audre Rapoport
Foundation
rapoportfdn.org

Heifer International
heifer.org

The Page Education Foundation
page-ed.org

Read to Feed
readtofeed.org

Ubuntu Education Fund
ubuntufund.org

U.S. Green Building Council
usgbc.org

BOOKS

McBrier, Page, illustrated by Lori
Lohstoeter. *Beatrice's Goat*.
New York: Atheneum, 2001.

8: Model Gifts

WEB SITES

The Abyssinian Development
Corporation
http://www.adcorp.org

African Development
Foundation
adf.gov

The American India Foundation
http://www.aifoundation.org

America's Promise Alliance
americaspromise.org

AmeriCorps
americorps.org

Central Asia Institute
ikat.org

CHF International
chfinternational.org

Clinton-Hunter Development
Initiative
clintonfoundation.org

College Track
collegetrack.org

The Covenant with Black
America
covenantwithblackamerica.com

The Greater Allen A.M.E.
Cathedral of New York
allencathedral.org

H.O.P.E. (Help Other People
Endure)
southafricanhope.org

The Hunter Foundation
thehunterfoundation.co.uk

Liberia Enterprise Development
Fund
http://www.chfhq.org/content/
general/detail/4614

Resources

Local Initiatives Support
Corporation
lisc.org

Millennium Promise
millenniumpromise.org

Overseas Private Investment
Corporation
opic.gov

Partners In Health
pih.org

Pennies for Peace
penniesforpeace.org

The U.N. Millennium
Development Goals
http://www.un.org/
millenniumgoals

The Urban Enterprise Initiative
clintonfoundation.org

BOOKS

Maxwell, Janine. *It's Not Okay with Me*. Enumclaw, Wash.: Winepress Publishing, 2006.

Mortenson, Greg, and David Oliver Relin. *Three Cups of Tea: One Man's Mission to Fight Terrorism and Build Nations*. New York: Viking, 2006.

Sachs, Jeffrey D. *The End of Poverty*. New York: Penguin Press, 2005.

Smiley, Tavis. *The Covenant with Black America*. Chicago: Third World Press, 2006.

Smiley, Tavis. *The Covenant in Action*. Carlsbad, Calif.: Smiley Books, 2007.

9: Giving to Good Ideas

WEB SITES

Annie E. Casey Foundation
http://www.aecg.org

Ashoka
ashoka.org

The Beehive
thebeehive.org

Cell Bazaar
corp.cellbazaar.com

CircleLending
circlelending.com

Common Sense Media
commonsensemedia.org

Daniel Pearl Foundation
danielpearl.org

Echoing Green Foundation
echoinggreen.org

Ford Foundation
fordfound.org

GlobalGiving
globalgiving.com

Harlem Children's Zone
hcz.org

KaBOOM!
kaboom.org

The Making Headway Foundation
makingheadway.org

Modest Needs
modestneeds.org

Nick Webber Trust
nickwebbertrust.dynalias.org

Omidyar Network
omidyar.net

One Economy
one-economy.com

Resources

Rory Peck Trust
rorypecktrust.org

Schwab Foundation for Social
Entrepreneurship
schwabfound.org

Sustainable South Bronx
ssbx.org

The THEA Foundation
theafoundation.org

World Economic Forum
http://www.weforum.org

BOOKS

Bornstein, David. *How to Change
the World: Social Entrepreneurs
and the Power of New Ideas.*
New York: Oxford University
Press, 2004.

10: *Organizing Markets*

WEB SITES

Cleantech Network
cleantech.com

Fair Trade Certified Coffee
Alliance
transfairusa.org

GE Ecomagination
ge.ecomagination.com

Global Fairness Initiative
globalfairness.org

Inter-American Development
Bank
http://www.iadb.org

Khosla Ventures
khoslaventures.com

Magic Johnson Foundation
magicjohnson.org

Pew Center on Global Climate
Change
pewclimate.org

Rocky Mountain Institute
rmi.org

Sanyo Think GAIA
sanyo.com/thinkgaia

The Solar Electric Light Fund
self.org

Trade Aid
tradeaid.uk.org

Virgin Earth Challenge
http://www.virginearth.com

World Economic Forum
http://www.weforum.org

X PRIZE Foundation
xprize.org

BOOKS

Brown, Lester R. *Eco-Economy.*
New York: W. W. Norton,
2001.

Brown, Lester R. *Plan B 2.0:
Rescuing a Planet Under Stress
and a Civilization in Trouble.*
New York: W. W. Norton,
2006.

Dunning, John H., ed. *Making
Globalization Good.* New York:
Oxford University Press, 2003.

Flannery, Tim. *The Weather
Makers: How Man Is Changing
the Climate and What It Means
for Life on Earth.* New York:
Atlantic Monthly Press, 2006.

Gore, Al. *Earth in the Balance:
Ecology and the Human Spirit.*
Boston: Houghton Mifflin,
1992.

Resources

Gore, Al. *An Inconvenient Truth: The Planetary Emergency of Global Warming and What We Can Do About It*. Emmaus, Pa.: Rodale Press, 2006.

Hart, Stuart L. *Capitalism at the Crossroads*. 2nd ed. Upper Saddle River, N.J.: Wharton School, 2007.

Hawken, Paul, Amory Lovins, and L. Hunter Lovins. *Natural Capitalism: Creating the Next Industrial Revolution*. Boston: Little, Brown and Co., 1999.

Leggett, Jeremy K. *The Empty Tank: Oil, Gas, Hot Air, and the Coming Global Financial Catastrophe*. New York: Random House, 2005.

Lovins, Amory B., E. Kyle Datta, Odd-Even Bustnes, Jonathan G. Koomey, and Nathan J. Glasgow. *Winning the Oil Endgame*. Snowmass, Colo.: Rocky Mountain Institute, 2004.

Porritt, Jonathon. *Capitalism: As If the World Matters*. Sterling, Va.: Earthscan, 2005.

Stiglitz, Joseph E., and Andrew Charlton. *Fair Trade for All*. New York: Oxford University Press, 2005.

Trask, Crissy. *It's Easy Being Green: A Handbook for Earth-Friendly Living*. Salt Lake City, Utah: Gibbs Smith, 2006.

Wood, Donna G., Jeanne M. Logsdon, Patsy G. Lewellyn, and Kim Davenport. *Global Business Citizenship: A Transformative Framework for Ethics and Sustainable Capitalism*. Armonk, N.Y.: M.E. Sharpe, 2006.

11: Nonprofit Markets

WEB SITES

C40 Cities—Climate Leadership Group
c40cities.org

Clinton Climate Initiative
clintonfoundation.org

Clinton Foundation HIV/AIDS Initiative
clintonfoundation.org

Clinton-Hunter Development Initiative
clintonfoundation.org

The Hunter Foundation
thehunterfoundation.co.uk

UNITAID
http://www.unitaid.eu/en/

BOOKS

Conroy, Anne C., ed., with a preface by Bono. *Poverty, AIDS and Hunger: Breaking the Poverty Trap in Malawi*. London: Palgrave Macmillan, 2007.

World Bank Country Study. *Education in Rwanda: Rebalancing Resources to Accelerate Post-Conflict Development and Poverty Reduction*. Washington, D.C.: World Bank Publications, 2003.

12: What About Government?

WEB SITES

AARP
aarp.org

ACORN
acorn.org

Resources

Better Health Care Together
betterhealthcaretogether.org

Bread for the World
bread.org

Catholics in Alliance for the
Common Good
catholicsinalliance.org

Center for American Progress
americanprogress.org

Center for Responsible Lending
responsiblelending.org

Ceres
ceres.org

Energy Entrepreneurs Network
green-alliance.org.uk

Environmental Defense
environmentaldefense.org

Faith in Public Life
faithinpubliclife.org

Families USA
familiesusa.org

The GAVI Alliance
gavialliance.org

The Global Fund to Fight AIDS,
Tuberculosis, and Malaria
theglobalfund.org

Greenpeace
greenpeace.org

The International Monetary Fund
imf.org

Mo Ibrahim Foundation
http://www.moibrahimfoundation
.org

National Breast Cancer Coalition
http://www.natlbcc.org

National Council of Churches
USA
ncccusa.org

National Geographic's *The Green
Guide*
thegreenguide.com

National Prostate Cancer
Coalition
fightprostatecancer.org

Natural Resources Defense
Council
nrdc.org

NextEnergy
nextenergy.org

ninemillion.org
ninemillion.org

ONE Campaign
one.org

Prostate Cancer Foundation
prostatecancerfoundation.org

The Sierra Club
sierraclub.org

Sojourners
sojo.net

TechTown
techtownwsu.org

UNICEF
unicef.org

UNITAID
http://www.unitaid.eu/en/

United Nations
http://www.un.org

United Nations Foundation
unfoundation.org

U.S. Mayors Climate Protection
Agreement
usmayors.org/climateprotection

The Women Waging Peace
Network
womenwagingpeace.net

The World Bank
worldbank.org

Resources

The World Health Organization
who.int

Yahoo! for Good
brand.yahoo.com/forgood

BOOKS

Supply Chain Saves the World.
Boston: AMR Research, 2006.

Edwards, Michael. *Civil Society.*
Malden, Mass.: Polity Press,
2004.

Hunt, Swanee. *This Was Not Our
War: Bosnian Women
Reclaiming the Peace.* Durham,
N.C.: Duke University Press,
2004.

Karoff, Peter, with Jane Maddox.
*The World We Want: New
Dimensions in Philanthropy and
Social Change.* Lanham, Md.:
AltaMira Press, 2007.

Pahl, Greg. *The Citizen-Powered
Energy Handbook.* White River
Junction, Vt.: Chelsea Green
Publishing, 2007.

Vaitheeswaran, Vijay V. *Power to
the People: How the Coming
Energy Revolution Will
Transform an Industry, Change
Our Lives, and Maybe Even Save
the Planet.* New York: Farrar,
Straus and Giroux, 2003.

13: How Much / Why?

WEB SITES

American Jewish World Service
ajws.org

Anti-Defamation League
adl.org

Inner-City Muslim Action
Network
imancentral.org

Jewish Charities of America
http://www.jewishcoa.org

MAZON
mazon.org

United Jewish Appeal
uja.org

World Vision International
worldvision.org

INDEX

AARP, 191
Abraham, Danny, 81, 96
Abyssinian Baptist Church, 130
Abyssinian Development Corporation
(ADC), 130
Aceh, 106, 171
ACORN (Association of Community
Organizations for Reform Now),
51–2, 79, 193
affordable housing, 125, 130
Afghanistan, 27–8, 84, 90, 94, 124, 125,
194
Africa, 6, 17, 18, 20, 22, 36, 39, 57, 60,
61, 93, 94, 110, 113, 117–18, 119,
120, 166, 183–4, 188, 210
HIV/AIDS in, 17, 20, 41–5, 58,
116–17, 121, 135
promotion of good governance in,
200
see also specific African nations
African Union, 201
after-school programs, 25, 80
Agaseke K'amaho Ro, 98
Agassi, Andre, 75
agriculture programs, 109–14, 119,
120–1, 123, 134, 135, 182
AIDS, *see* HIV/AIDS
Alabama, 18, 107
Alaska, 155
Albright, Madeleine, 86, 93
Alcoholics Anonymous, 101
Alliance for a Healthier Generation,
37, 38
Amalgamated Bank, 177
America Learns, 71
American Bar Association, xi
American Beverage Association, 183
American Heart Association, 19, 30,
37, 38

American Indian Foundation (AIF),
133–4
American Jewish World Service, 208
America Reads, 70, 71
America's Promise, 132–3
AmeriCorps, 32, 45, 126, 175
Amnesty International, 11
Amoils, Maya, 134–5
amputees, 22
Amsterdam, 163
Andre Agassi College Preparatory
Academy, 73–5
Angels in Africa (Sevcik and
O'Donnell), 98
Angkor Hospital for Children, 22
Animal Rescue New Orleans, 30–1
Annan, Kofi, 107, 118
Annie E. Casey Foundation, 101, 142
Anti-Defamation League, 208
antiretroviral medications (ARVs),
20–1, 22, 40, 44, 180, 182
Arab League, 202
Arabs, 31, 89–92, 95, 96, 182
Araujo, Consuelo, 99
Archimedes Fund, 23
ARK (Absolute Return for Kids), 17
Arkansas, x, xi, 7, 18, 28, 72, 113, 147,
167, 168
Arkansas, University of, 46, 106
Arkansas Advocates for Children and
Families, xi
Arkansas Rice Depot, 67
Armstrong, Lance, 23–4, 86
Arunachalam, Jaya, 94–5
Ashoka, 138–40, 141
Asia, 39, 94, 110, 113, 158, 188
tsunami disaster of, 10, 13, 60, 68–9,
106, 107–8, 171, 209
Aspell, Mauria, 148

Index

Index

Index

Index

Index

Index

Index

Index

Murdoch, Rupert, 210
Murebwayire, Josephine, 96–7
musical instruments, 61–3
MusiCares, 61
Music Rising, 61–2
Mzalazala, Fezeka, 114

National Academy Foundation (NAF),
  77–8
National Black MBA Association, 127
National Breast Cancer Coalition
  (NBCC), 191
National Council of Churches, 193
National Geographic, 198
National Institutes of Health, 53
National Obesity Forum, 37–8
National Prostate Cancer Coalition,
  192
natural disasters, 20, 32, 45, 46, 50–3,
  60, 61–2, 79, 126, 171, 209
  gift-giving programs for, 68–9
  model gifts for, 133–4
  new beginning programs for, 105–8
  philanthropy for, 10, 13, 28, 30–1,
    69
Natural Resources Defense Council,
  190
NBA, 40
Nepal, 59, 112
new beginning programs, 101–8, 207
  for children of prison inmates,
    103–4
  for former prison inmates, 17, 47,
    101–6
  for homeless, 104–6
  for natural disasters, 105–8
New Hope for Cambodian Children,
  xii
New Markets Tax Credit, 126, 176
New Orleans, La., 45, 51–2, 61, 107,
  196
  see also Hurricane Katrina
New York, 28, 57, 66, 102
New York, N.Y., 39, 73, 127–30, 146,
  206
  environmental programs in, 146,
    197
  poverty and low-income
    communities in, 16–17, 145,
    176–7
  school programs in, 24–5, 116,
    143–4
New York State Fair, 10

New York University, 94
  Stern School of Business at, 127
New Zealand, 10, 63, 73
NextEnergy, 197–8
NGOs (nongovernmental
  organizations)
  for community development, 51–2,
    65, 80, 101–2, 106–8, 109–14,
    125–34, 131, 142–6, 176–7
  for education and schools, 6, 13–14,
    17–18, 24–5, 57–60, 61–3, 65,
    71–8, 124–5, 132, 133–6, 142–5,
    148–50
  for employment of low-income
    people, 17, 39, 48, 174–5
  for environmental protection and
    conservation, 156–61, 164, 167,
    189–90, 197–8
  for fair trade and labor standards,
    170–3, 184
  faith-based, 47–9, 60, 65, 106,
    188–9, 208
  for funding social entrepreneurs,
    137–51
  gift-giving programs of, 56–7,
    58–67
  for health care and medicine, 13–14,
    22–3, 56–7, 65, 190–2, 202
  for health and fitness, 12, 37–40, 81
  for HIV/AIDs health care, xiii, 5–6,
    14–15, 20–1, 22, 34–6, 41–5,
    116–17, 178–82
  for improving governance in
    developing nations, 8, 12,
    199–203
  as microcredit and mortgage
    lenders, 6–8, 9, 20, 27–8, 51,
    78–80, 95, 121
  model programs of, 116–36
  for natural disasters, see natural
    disasters
  new beginning programs of, 101–8
  in nonprofit markets, 178–84
  philanthropy and charitable
    donations through, 19–24, 114,
    118–19
  for poverty, see poverty
  in public good markets, 152–78
  reconciliation programs of, 88–98
  skills-giving programs of, 70–87
  for women's rights, 93–5, 110, 200
  by young people, 28–30
  see also specific NGOs

235

Index

Index

Index